IT'S 6 A.M. & I'M ALREADY BEHIND!

30 Strategies to Get Caught Up In a Crazy-Busy World!

LAUREN MIDGLEY

It's 6am and I am Already Behind: 30 Strategies to Get Caught Up in a Crazy-Busy World!

Lauren Midgley

Copyright ©2015

All rights reserved

Published by Focused Action Publishing

P. O. Box 1072

Colleyville, Texas 76034

Printed in the United States of America

FIRST EDITION

Cover design by Dawn Teagarden

ISBN 978-0-9889518-7-7

The examples used in this book are real-life examples from my own consulting clients. However, because I have a strict code of confidentiality with all my clients, the examples use different names than the actual or potentially identifying information has been changed to honor that commitment.

What Others are Saying About Lauren Midgley & Her Strategies

"This book is a must have for anyone looking to change their mindset on productivity in this busy world. Lauren Midgley wants you to stop setting yourself up to fail. Instead, she wants you to "win" every day at being productive."

—**James Malinchak,** Featured on ABC's Hit TV Show, "Secret Millionaire" and Founder, www.MillionaireFreeBook.com

"We all complain that we never have enough time to do what we really want to do. Lauren Midgley wants you to focus in on "What matters most right NOW!" This book is a must-read to develop your time muscle and power productivity strategies."

—**Joe Calloway,** Author, Magnetic: The Art of Attracting Business

"This valuable book is chock full of easy, practical and smart ideas on how to get caught up! Feeling productive every day adds to our well-being. Thank you, Lauren, for this valuable information!"

—**Joel Boggess,** Best-selling Author and Syndicated Radio Host

"Let's change the workplace and home life by being realistic on our productivity. We all have things to do —some important, some not-so-important. Lauren Midgley's book helps us to focus on "What matters most right NOW!"

—**Eric Lofholm,** President, Eric Lofholm International

"Winners understand better than anyone else how crucial being productive is. My friend Lauren Midgley introduces you to 30 winning ideas for being more productive. She challenges you to stop giving up on yourself and provides the tools you need to live your life powerfully. Grab your to do list. And make this book your top priority."

—**Dan Waldschmidt,** best selling author & champion ultra-runner

Motivate and Inspire Others!
Share This Book

Retail $24.95

Special Quantity Discounts

5-20 Books	$21.95
21-99 Books	$18.95
100-499 Books	$15.95
500-999 Books	$10.95
1,000+ Books	$8.95

To place an order, contact:

817-965-4244

www.its6ambook.com

www.LaurenMidgley.com

info@LaurenMidgley.com

The Ideal Speaker for Your Next Event

For any organization that wants to maximize productivity and profitability, then hire Lauren for a keynote and/or workshop training.

To contact or book Lauren to speak:

Courage to Succeed Consulting
P. O. Box 1072
Colleyville, TX 76034

817-965-4244

info@LaurenMidgley.com
www.LaurenMidgley.com
www.its6ambook.com

Also by Lauren Midgley

Masterminding Our Way: The Power of 5 Minds
Create your own mastermind group to create ideas,
learn new perspectives, and experience breakthroughs

Successfully Failing at Procrastination
A proven step-by-step process to impact
your procrastination habit

This Book is Dedicated to:

This book is dedicated to those who want to improve their productivity, without spending MORE time. Rather, they are passionate about using their precious time in a way that serves their life and serves others. By so doing, they create the calm, balanced world around them, feeling accomplished every day.

It is time to get caught up. The feeling of always "being behind" weighs heavily on your happiness and peace with life.

To my kids, Anne and JP, who are ardent supporters — I love you both so much. I am very proud of your accomplishments every day. I appreciate your belief in me as your mom.

To Don, my true love, thank you for your unwavering support through this journey. Words do not adequately describe how much you mean to me.

To Scott, my brother, I love you and enjoy your spirit of getting things done in routine fashion!

To Shari, my sister, I love you and so appreciate your way of being focused on the important tasks to do.

To James Malinchak, thank you for being my coach and understanding my journey. You are an amazing individual who has helped so many share their voice and gifts with the world.

The Reality

Yes, it is 6 a.m. and I am already behind.

It is 6 p.m. and I am still not done and cannot leave work.

It is 11 p.m. and I cannot shut off my swirling mind to go to sleep.

*It is 3 a.m. and I am now awake thinking
about all the things I need to do.*

These words were my life.
It was a never-ending cycle.

I knew it had to stop. I was overwhelmed. I was frustrated. My life felt like the words "rinse and repeat" we see on shampoo bottles.

Go to work, come home, eat dinner, play with the kids, find five minutes of "me" time, go to sleep. Do it again. Again and again.

In the fantasy world that lived in my head was the life I wanted:

Yes, it is 6 a.m. and I am refreshed and ready to take on the day, excited for all the things ahead of me.

It is 6 p.m. and I leave the office, knowing that I have accomplished what I needed to do for that day.

It is 11 p.m. and I welcome sleep to close out the day.

It is 3 a.m. and I enjoy my restorative sleep.

I so wanted to feel caught up…just once.

Am I describing your life, too?

How did this happen to us?

What did we allow?

Why do we tolerate this life?

Are there no boundaries?

What Does Feeling Caught Up Look Like?

The difference in the two scenarios is feeling caught up or truly being caught up. Having the mindset to be productive and accept what can or cannot be accomplished that day. Our self-talk matters.

In this book, I introduce you to the concept of The Productive Mind™, which confronts the new norms of feeling behind and overwhelmed, the trap of "superficial productivity" and the toll of our "runaway expectations" impacting our emotional and physical health.

I discovered a quote about fifteen years ago that speaks to me every day. I have shared it with thousands of people in the workplace, in my workshops, during my keynote presentations, in Toastmaster clubs—and anyone else who would listen.

Ralph Waldo Emerson, a nineteenth-century poet, essayist, and philosopher, was known for his quotes about daily life, nature, and ethical living. He captures the essence of what is important as we shift our thinking on productivity.

"Finish each day and be done with it.

You have done what you could.

Some blunders and absurdities no doubt crept in;
forget them as soon as you can.

Tomorrow is a new day; begin it well and serenely and with too
high a spirit to be encumbered with your old nonsense."

The power of consistency in our lives does make a difference. It is the small, consistent steps that have an impact in the long run. This quote speaks to the paradox of change and routine.

> *"Miss only a couple weeks of anything — workouts at the gym, affectionate gestures toward your spouse, or the phone calls that are part of your prospecting routine — and you don't just lose the results those two weeks would have produced. If that's all you lost (which is what most people assume), not much damage would be done. But by slacking off for even a short time, you killed Mo. It's dead. And that is a tragedy."*
> —**Darren Hardy,** *The Compound Effect*

> *"You will never change your life until you change something you do on a daily basis. The secret of your success is found in your daily routine."*
> —**John Maxwell,** *The 15 Invaluable Laws of Growth*

And finally, the people around you who either build you up or tear you down do have an impact on your productive psyche.

> *"There comes a time in your life when you realize who matters, who never did, and who always will. So don't worry about people from your past because there is a reason why they didn't make it to your future."*
> —**Adam Lindsay Gordon,** *Australian poet, jockey and politician*

Contents

It is About Getting Caught Up and Staying That Way

Let's Start with the Words "Courage to Succeed"

My year in 2010 started out with the words "Courage to Succeed" playing over and over in my head. I did not know why. I would soon find out very quickly.

The bedside chats in January with my mom, who was dying of cancer, were filled with discussions centered around the concept of "What Matters Most Right Now." She was an active participant in hearing about my career, my relationships, and my challenges. She frequently commented that I needed to focus on what matters most right now.

At that time, I was very busy in my corporate job with traveling, motivating an awesome team, raising a family as a single mom, and on some days just surviving. Every third weekend, I traveled to Florida to spend a long weekend with her, knowing that her days were numbered. It was as though I wanted to cram as much of her wisdom into my head as I could.

I **never** felt caught up in my personal or business life. I felt like I always had this weight hanging over my head that could drop at any time to crush me. I always had things to do. I was never, ever caught up. That would have been nirvana!

Do you ever feel like that?

I would wake up in the mornings hearing these words in my head: Courage to Succeed.

"Lauren, you need the courage to succeed. You can do this. Have the courage to succeed."

I knew that the word origin of courage was French for "coeur," which means heart. High standards and success were words that lived in my life on an everyday basis. I asked myself every day, "What do I need to do today to achieve success?"

Mom passed away in late January 2010.

A series of events began to unfold over the next few months. My son suffered a very serious broken leg. I experienced what I perceived at the time to be public humiliation while speaking on stage at my company's annual event. A family member had a drug addiction relapse. It was all happening in rapid-fire progression.

No matter how many hours I worked, I was never caught up. I groaned every morning at my desk as I added more and more tasks to the To Do list. Each day, I did accomplish some of those tasks, but not as many as I was adding. The weight of the world felt so heavy on my shoulders.

Life in all its glory was happening around me.

Courage to Succeed

The ringing of the words "Courage to Succeed" kept getting louder and louder.

Finally one day, I connected the dots to create a clearer picture. It hit me. Those words were to be my company name.

I was a bit puzzled, as I was still employed at the time. As I listened to the quiet voice in my head, I realized it was time to leave the corporate position. It was time to share my talents and gifts with the world.

◆ It was time to get caught up and feel differently.

◆ To feel better.

◆ To be in control. (are we ever in control?)

◆ To be happier.

◆ To have freedom.

As soon as I provided my resignation, I created a list of all the projects I was working on for my successor. The list astounded even me. Was I really working on that many things? No wonder I was exhausted, burned out and looking for an alternative.

The vision for my newly founded business: I was to help others with their courage to succeed. And along the way, I would find my courage to succeed. The puzzle picture was started to be clearer as more pieces went into place.

Now after five years later, it makes much more sense to me, as I have lived the "Courage to Succeed" way.

Through this book, I show you how being more productive enhances your confidence and courage. Your ownership of your productivity will serve you for many years. Many of us are not as productive as we would like. We struggle getting things done. We yearn for the simple life ... the simple way.

17

We want to be caught up with our work and our life.

Our world is moving at such a fast pace. Sometimes we wonder if we can keep up.

Sometimes we wonder, "How is everyone else keeping up, and I'm not?" "Are they caught up and I am the only one who is not?" We try to cram more into each day and wind up exhausted and not as effective.

Each day, we focus on a current task just to get it done and move onto the next one. Rinse and repeat. Over and over. It is no wonder we are frazzled, anxious, and not enjoying life as much as we would like.

I overheard a twenty-something make a comment to her friend. *"Yes, I am crushing my tasks. But, why am I going through life like this? It doesn't matter how hard you work, how fast you do things. Eventually, it doesn't matter."*

I shake my head at statements like the ones she said. My realization is that everyone approaches productivity with a different frame of reference. As schoolkids, we did not learn time management from a class. Instead, it was each individual figuring out their own productivity pace.

Strengthsfinder® Top Strength

One of my top five strengths in the Gallup StrengthsFinder® is that of an Activator. Here is an excerpt from my Signature Theme about Activators:

"When can we start?" This is a recurring question in your life. You are impatient for action. You may concede that analysis has its uses or that debate and discussion can occasionally yield some valuable insights, but deep down you know that only <u>action is real</u>. Only action can make things happen. Only action leads to performance. Once a decision is

made, you <u>cannot not act</u>."

"You know that you will be judged not by what you say, not by what you think, but by what you get done. This <u>does not frighten you. It pleases you</u>." [Underlining added by me]

Tying this all together is my mantra: **Having the courage to succeed, I know that action is real. I must act. Once a decision is made, I cannot not act. I am not fearful to make things happen."**

My Earlier Story

My first awareness of why focused productivity matters came to me when I was thirty years old. I had just moved to the Philadelphia area for a much-sought-after promotion. As I reflected on my relationship with time, I discovered my most productive time of the day is 6 a.m. to 8 a.m. It became my life long pattern of highly productive time. If I needed an occasional burst to get more work done, I would get started even earlier at 4:30 a.m. or 5 a.m.

Thus, during my work career, I would go to the office around 5:30 or so, to be ready for my "productive time" to get the day started. As you can imagine, there are not many people in the building at that time who are working. So those of us crazy enough to be there that early quickly found out who else was as crazy. It was the "Early-Bird Breakfast Club." The crazy people who liked to work and were focused on getting it done.

A wonderful man named Carmen was one of the company's chief accountants. He was one of those crazy early birds. Carmen was a conscientious employee. He cared about others, and he had been with the company longer than I had. He was Italian, born in Philly, and loved telling stories. Being new to the area and this role, I lacked confidence. Early on, Carmen befriended me. Soon, I felt very comfortable with him, his viewpoints, and his authenticity.

A side note to the story is that there are a few unwritten rules amongst the early-bird crowd. The first rule is that you are not there to chat with the other early birds, but rather you are there for a purpose, which is to get work done.

The second unwritten rule is that the first one into the office **always makes the coffee.** Remember that this timeframe was in the days before Starbucks. You either made your coffee at home or drank it at work. Or both.

I remember one early morning quite vividly. I had just been promoted to a regional vice-president role, under Victor, my boss who was the company's president. I was spending many extra hours to learn my new job. I would review files to see what my predecessors had done and do research about my region, so I would be fully up to speed.

My desk was a mess. I had papers and files all over it. Carmen passed by my office many mornings. He saw my chaos. One morning, he knocked on the open door and asked if he could come in.

He sat down in the chair in front of my desk. I knew my caring "Italian big brother" had just arrived to share with me, the little sister, the philosophy of how things worked.

His first words were "Lauren, how do you know if you are successful at this role? What are your measurements? What results are you trying to achieve? Has Victor clearly defined his vision of success for you in this role? What are the key areas you need to spend your time on?"

I sat there wide-eyed. So many questions in such a short time. My head was spinning. Essentially, he was asking me, "Do you know what the priorities to be worked on are?" To me at the age of 30, everything felt like a priority.

No one, in my short nine years of the workplace after college, had been that clear or concise about the relationship of time and results. If the other bosses along the way had done so, I had not remembered it or applied it.

He continued. "You will not be judged if you have all your paperwork done ... but rather what you achieve in your position and the results you deliver. If you are working from 6 a.m. to 5 p.m., make sure you are working on the right things to impact results."

I visibly gulped and nodded.

"One more thing—you need to be very clear on what the picture of success looks like. Without that vision, you will be working hard but working blind."

The lesson he shared in the space of fifteen minutes had an incredible impact on me and how I viewed my role. I now knew that I needed to use my time more wisely to lead the team of twelve people, many of whom were older than I.

Our Work Pattern

His words also set up the longtime pattern of how I viewed the time I needed to spend doing my work each day. My normal workday started at 6 a.m. and ended at 6 p.m. or later.

Of course, no one from the company or my boss chided me for working four more hours each day than was required. In the '80s, it was customary to work more hours than the standard forty. In fact, it was a status symbol. Those who left at 5 p.m. were frowned upon.

It wasn't until I had the conversation with Carmen that I understood the connection of time spent with maximum results. It seemed very normal to me to go in two hours before the rest of the employees and stay at least one or two hours after everyone had left.

I wanted to be viewed as productive and getting results. I valued Carmen's advice at the time. However, the information he provided did not override my belief system. My beliefs were that to get results, you worked harder and spent more time to do the required tasks. I never felt caught up.

The dot that I did not connect for quite some time was the concept of working efficiently to get results. That mastery came many years later.

Connection Between Time and Results

This year, I met a woman who works for Southwestern Publishing, based out of Nashville, Tennessee. She is the adult leader of the young adults' summer internship program. I attended a parents' meeting, where she discussed the activities our young-adult children will be doing for their summer internship program.

As she explained the details, I heard a comment that hit me hard between the eyes. Here is what she said (paraphrased by me):

> *For their whole lives, we have told our children they can be all that they want to be. We have told them they can do anything in life. But as they begin the march into the work world, how do they really know they can do or be anything?*
>
> *But how do **they** really know what they can do?*
>
> *(this question was the comment that packed the punch for me)*
>
> *How have they been pushed to the limits to test their "get it done" ability and truly get results?*

As she said those words, I reflected on my own path of how I have either set my intention to accomplish a task, or series of tasks, and then either succeeded or failed.

I just kept working to check off the "done" box.

Or did I just keep working to stay ahead, in an attempt to be caught up?

How have I modeled that for my son? What has he learned from me about getting things done?

What she was really saying to us, as parents, was that through our personal accomplishments, we build confidence and determination.

Her message is a powerful one for young adults (my son at age twenty) and for older adults.

It reminds me of another example: In April 2012, I spoke to a group of job seekers about the impact of procrastination. My message to them was focused on overcoming this habit for two main reasons.

First, the habit of procrastination was impacting the results of their job search. Their self-talk was talking them into not taking the right actions. The results of their lack of action impacted their home life, relationships, finances, and self-worth.

Second, it was worthwhile to overcome this habit while they were in the job search, so that when they were hired, the habit would not impact their job performance.

During that presentation, I collected contact information from those who were interested in attending my workshop to dig in deeper on busting through this habit. I did not obtain contact information from everyone.

Interestingly enough, three years later in April 2015, I received an e-mail from a gentleman who was part of that group. He was at his wit's end with his job search and his poor habits. He wrote to say that he felt horrible that he has been out of work since 2009, affecting his family life and the relationships around him. I could feel his despair in his words.

The anguish I read in his e-mail reinforced for me that this habit can be devastating if not addressed.

It **does** matter that we gain confidence, know our strengths, and can accomplish what is important to us at the time. When those three factors **don't** happen, then we find fault with life, ourselves, and others. This gentleman has many fears stopping him from taking action. He is stuck.

As I reflected on the e-mail received from this job seeker, the question I would ask him: "Is the comfort zone that you are stuck in really that comfortable?" In this situation, he is:

◆ uncomfortable where he is—doing nothing

◆ uncomfortable to be vulnerable

◆ uncomfortable to face the actions he needs to take

I believe none of those options are very comfortable for him. He has already picked one that is not serving him — doing nothing. What actions can he take that will lead him to a different, and more satisfying result?

My Goal for You

I hope this book will offer you some insight about **your** productive mind, so that you accomplish what needs to be done, reduce your overwhelm and feel good about yourself.

> The Productive Mind™ is a beneficial outlook on one's daily approach, a deliberate and focused way of thinking about accomplishment and personal satisfaction.

How you approach your productivity is very personal and highly individualized. I have created a productivity framework based on what has worked for my clients and what has not worked.

My intent is to disrupt your thinking enough for you to consider other possibilities. I want you to think about how to be more productive at home and at work, without throwing more time at the situation. The easy answer to getting more done is to spend more time. The harder answer is figuring out how to get more done in less time.

I think the time we have today is precious, our most treasured commodity.

Your personal productivity affects everything you do: your well-being, your relationships, your wealth, your health.

Each of the six chapters will unfold a broad concept, key points, and examples. I encourage you to highlight, take notes, or journal your impressions. The information is designed to poke at your thinking and encourage you to try out new concepts.

Thoughts on Time Management

I challenge you to consider this: Why do time-management techniques not work over the long haul?

We try them for a while and go back to our old ways. Why does that happen?

I believe that when you adopt a time-management technique that you also have to adopt a mind shift to make it stick. Remember my Carmen example? I heard the words he said, but I did not shift my mind or behavior at that time.

This book is about your mind shift. Your productive mind shifting to a higher level of performance. Why would we want to do that? The four major benefits are:

1. Happiness
2. Confidence
3. Less stress
4. Enjoy life much more

To achieve those benefits in your life, you will want to consider these thirty strategies to impact your life. Some will work for you; some may not. Some you have heard of and will appreciate the reminder; others will be a fresh perspective.

This book takes you through a step-by-step process embodied in six chapters. The first one starts with challenging you to consider your **current** relationship with time. Establishing what is your starting point as of now.

The next step is the realization that time is simply…. time. The clock will keep ticking regardless whether you are caught up or not.

Whether you realize it or not, you use a few time management techniques on a daily basis that you have learned work for you. However, it is important to have a set of Daily Non-Negotiables that guide your productivity in an intentional way.

I love the phrases we use in our everyday language about time. In fact, I was so amused by the number of common phrases that I created a exhaustive, but fun list of them located in the Appendix section. For example, we all know that we cannot "make time" or "manage time". Time is time. How we use the minutes matters, but we cannot alter the ticking of the clock.

Every day, we have things to do. Knowing why we do these things and how well we do them is important to know. The "things" we do can take a specific amount of time from a quick single task to a drawn-out multitask project. How we approach these tasks and our pace does matter.

As with anything in life, there are times when we want to make an immediate difference in getting things done and being caught up.

The benefits of better personal productivity can pay off huge dividends in feeling caught up and not being behind. To do so, you will want to determine what tweaks are needed in your schedule to intentionally make that will make a difference.

And finally, information is only information unless you take action and implement in your life. Mastering the information means that you have learned it, applied it and improved it. That takes time.

Let's get started. We have no time to waste.

Lauren

YOUR
RELATIONSHIP
WITH TIME

"Don't mistake movement for achievement.
It's easy to get faked out by being busy.
The question is busy doing what."

—Jim Rohn, American entrepreneur,
author and motivational speaker

As we begin on this journey of looking at time and productivity, first note that we all have an inner clock that dictates our relationship with time. Fast; slow. Proactive; reactive. Controlled; uncontrolled.

Some of us are wired to move fast, some wired to move slower. One who is wired to move fast will have a difficult time in slowing that inner clock down. And vice versa.

There are parts of our day where we proactively decide how we use our time—other parts where we are reactive to situations and others.

Our perception of control may be distorted. We may think we control our time, but do we?

We know that we all have the same amount of time. Some of us use it more productively than others. How does that happen?

Those who use time effectively and efficiently seem to be happier, be less stressed, and get more done to lead better lives. Is that really true?

What is the difference between a person who appears to always be on task and accomplish huge results and a person who struggles and seems to never get anything done?

Regardless of the phase of life we're in, the people are around us, and our workplace, our inner clock has its own metronome. The definition of a metronome from Dictionary.com is *a mechanical or electrical instrument that makes repeated clicking sounds at an **adjustable** pace, used for marking rhythm, especially in practicing music.*

I made the key word bold: **adjustable.** Our pace is predetermined by our inner clock.

Our day-to-day challenge is aligning our inner clock with the actual clock. When they are out of alignment, we feel overwhelmed and too busy.

Starting with Your Belief System

"Four steps to achievement: Plan purposefully,
prepare prayerfully, proceed positively,
pursue persistently."
—William A. Ward, American author

If you think back on how you learned about time and productivity, then likely you'll realize that you observed others and how they handled time. Our role models were our parents, our teachers, our bosses, our spouses, and our friends.

We adopted a belief about time. A quote from the great football coach Vince Lombardi, "If you are early, you are on time. If you are on time, you are late. If you are late, don't bother showing up." Some individuals will relate to that statement, with their personality being more driven by time. Others will think that quote is a ridiculous statement.

Richard, a guy I worked with, would always chuckle when I would call **in advance** to let him know when I was going to be five minutes late. In his world, being late meant fifteen to thirty minutes after the appointment time. The reality was that if I showed up five minutes late, he would not have cared or noticed. If I am meeting someone and they are five minutes late, I am highly aware and consulting the clock.

Clearly, we had different beliefs about time.

Other beliefs come into play. You might be able to relate to these statements.

- ◆ "I need big blocks of time to get a big project done."
- ◆ "I have too much to do every day."
- ◆ "I cannot accomplish much in a fifteen-minute time slot."
- ◆ "I don't get anything done because I am always distracted."

If you are not as productive as you would like, then your first thought might be to sign up for a time-management class. You would learn techniques, probably use them for a week or two, and then most likely go back to your original way of doing things without long-term impact.

In general, our minds do not like big projects with many steps. The same goes for long-term goals that we find difficult to impact on a day-to-day basis. When you are twenty, it is hard to think about and plan for retirement funds that you'll need at age sixty-eight. Forty-eight years seems so far away, so why take action today?

The best strategy for long-term impact is to become self-aware about how you view time and to understand your belief system, as it relates to daily time, weekly time, and yearly time.

*It is all about your productive mind-set; it is **not** about the clock.*

 # Example

Kathryn had been known for being late her entire life. This pattern impacted her close relationships, her work, her family ... every aspect of her life.

She was unable to commit to a specific time.

As you can imagine, her lack of being able to manage herself relative to time impacted everything and everyone in her world. She was highly frustrated with herself and the reactions of those around her.

She had tried many different techniques for being on time, from setting the alarm earlier to reducing the number of tasks she had to do.

What finally worked was to shift her mind-set, with my help. The way we accomplished that involved two important concepts.

1. Change her belief system to include the statement that she **could** be on time. It hard for Kathryn to make this change because she had resigned herself to not working on this habit. She did make the commitment.

2. Celebrate the success when she was on time.

Kathryn started each day by asking herself these four questions:

1. What steps do I need to take to be successfully on time all day today?

2. In this hour, what is the most important task I must accomplish?

3. What distractions will occur today that must I ignore?

4. What activity do I need to wrap up, without convincing myself to start something else?

What delayed her was the thought that she could do more than was physically possible. For example, she would begin to get ready for work. While doing that, she would walk by the laundry basket and decide to throw in a load of wash. Then, she would engage in watching TV, rather than getting ready for work.

Both activities were not helping her stay on track with the task she needed to focus on, which was getting ready for work. People like Kathryn will consistently **underestimate how long it takes to complete a task.**

To answer the first question, she began to understand the connection of how much could she truly accomplish. There were some days where she had limited capacity of time and had to limit her belief of what could be done.

She asked herself the second question every hour on the hour. I counseled her that her answer should be no more than three things.

At 7 a.m. in the morning, she needed to get ready for work. It was not the time to watch TV or to do laundry.

The third question is a reality check on what type of distractions impact us. Some are more manageable than others. Determine which you can control and which ones cause delays. The impact of electronics in our lives can wreak havoc. Checking your phone six to ten times per hour will slow down productivity.

The fourth question for Kathryn dealt with starting too many projects all at once or at inappropriate times. Once she realized that she needed to be more purposeful in finishing up what she started, her mindset and belief system began to shift.

Overcoming the Case Of the "I Do Not Want To's"

"Success is the ability to go from failure to failure
without losing your enthusiasm."

—Winston Churchill, British Prime Minister

Most of us procrastinate when we do not want to do an unpleasant task.

It doesn't matter what time it is or how long it will take to do the task. If we don't want to do it, then we are likely to postpone getting it done.

Consider how much less guilt and stress you would feel if you just completed the task.

Are you spending more time thinking about not wanting to do it than it would take to just do it? Usually this is the case.

With the Productive Mind™ in place, you are wanting to resolve this inner conflict. Identifying what is the real issue of your resistance will lead you to a better path of accomplishment.

The first step is to ask yourself: Why am I avoiding this task?

Most likely, there is anxiety and doubt surrounding how you feel about this task, fueling the resistance of completion.

Is this a one-time task that you do not want to do or a recurring task?

The second step is to ask yourself: What are the consequences I will face if I continue to delay?

The third step is to ask yourself: Are my feelings speaking louder than my logical desire to take action? Maybe you have done this task in the past, had unpleasant feelings about it then, and are unfairly associating those feelings now.

Once you have spent some time to analyze why you are not taking action, then it is time to set up your strategy.

The strategy that works is to encourage positive self-talk. Consider these words.

If I do this task now, then I know that a specific bad consequence will not happen.

I know how to do this task and whether I like it or not, it is time to do this task now or by a specific time today.

If I do this task, I will reward myself in the following way.

The part about this task I do not like is X, and I can ask person Y to help me.

*It is all about your productive mind-set; it is **not** about the clock.*

Example

I worked with a client, Tracy, who was a mobile therapist and saw clients in their homes. She loved seeing the clients. She hated completing the charts. Doing the paperwork was a required task of the job. She had no choice but to do it.

Instead of doing her chart at the client location or taking ten to fifteen minutes in the car after the client visit, Tracy would postpone this task until the weekend. By the time the weekend came, it was a gargantuan task.

She was unhappy, as was her family. They viewed her as working a full-time job during the week and then spending another six to eight hours of her free time on Sundays to do this task.

The solution seems obvious, but it can be hard to implement on a consistent basis.

First, she had to shift her mindset on how to approach this consistent task. Throughout the week, she never felt caught up. In reality, she wasn't caught up. This feeling contributed to her overwhelm on a daily basis.

Second, she needed to build time into her schedule to complete the charts after each visit. By doing so, she saw one less client each day. This change impacted her income, but altered how she felt about herself in a positive way.

Tracy began completing her chart immediately after her client visit.

What she found was that while the information was fresh in her mind, she could complete a chart in twenty to thirty minutes. When she waited until the weekend, it would take her forty-five to sixty minutes to review her notes, recall details in her mind, and eliminate the distractions that arose.

Restructuring her day to allow time to complete the task was much more efficient and productive. Her family was much happier, too.

She was caught up on a daily basis by making space in her schedule to complete the task in less time.

Staying Focused in an Unfocused World

"Living the unfocused life will lead
to the unfinished life."

—*Lauren Midgley, speaker, author,
business strategy consultant.*

By definition, unfocused is "without a specific aim or direction."

Many people are just wandering through each day, without intention. They have no goals or direction. They wake up each day, go to their jobs, go home, and do it all over again. Just as I described in my introduction, it is easy to fall into this time trap.

Others live a more intentional life. They know what they want to accomplish each day, week, month, this year, next year, or even the next five years.

So, how do we stay focused and become more intentional?

The strategy is to create an intentional mind-set that embraces the ability to focus on the tasks each day.

The Productive Mind™ confronts the challenges that occur in our daily life that de-focus us. The starting point is to make the choice that each day will be productive.

Next, you choose to be caught up with tasks in those areas that mean the most to you, for that specific day.

To make this happen, you will need tools to keep your productive mind on track. One way to do this is through purposeful visual reminders such as small sign or vision boards that have key words listed. I have a client that has her daily and weekly goal sheet in the front of her appointment book so that she is reminded throughout the day of her focus.

Another way to accomplish a heightened level of focus is through consistent planning at predetermined, specific intervals:

- ◆ 5 minutes each night
- ◆ 30 minutes end of each week on Friday afternoon
- ◆ 60 minutes each month on the last day
- ◆ ½ day each quarter
- ◆ 1 day each year

Why would we want to do this?

The consistency and intention will allow you to be more productive with what YOU want to accomplish. Regardless of what is going on around you in the unfocused world, you will stand out as a focused, intentional person. Taking to time to step away from the desk or piles of work provides your mind the chance to think more clearly.

The naysayers will tell you it is not possible. Don't listen. Become disciplined by putting the above planning times in your calendar. Try it for a ninety day period to see if you are more caught up through great intention.

*It is all about your productive mind-set; it is **not** about the clock.*

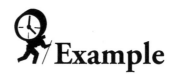

Example

One of my clients started a business with his wife over five years ago. Now, the business is generating a decent amount of revenue from a variety of products and services sold to a variety of industries.

A key question I asked the couple:

Of all the industries you serve, which one is the most profitable for you?

The question stopped them in their tracks. As they built their business, they would serve any paying customer from any industry. They had never thought to specialize in one type of industry or size of customer.

The next question was even more thought provoking.

What would happen if all your future new business came from that one industry, where you focused your marketing dollars and your salespeople's time? What would happen to your business if you were the "go-to experts" in the products and services needed by this one industry segment?

The reality was they had shaped their business in the first five years without an intentional, focused strategy. After considering my questions, they realized that the business would be much more efficient and profitable by focusing on their most profitable industry for the upcoming years.

Use focus to your advantage. Take time to think about your power questions to cause a shift in your thinking. The reality for this couple was that they were never caught up with their tasks because they were trying to serve too many industries. Their success came when they narrowed their business to two major industries. Their resources of time and people were now concentrated to deliver a greater return.

Identify Your Pattern with Time—It's About Mind-Set

"An idealist believes the short run doesn't count.
A cynic believes the long run doesn't matter. A realist
believes that what is done or left undone in the
short run determines the long run."

—*Sydney J. Harris, American journalist*

When are you the most productive? Do you work at certain times of the day or night more efficiently? Do you work in bursts, accomplishing a lot based on your focus and concentration? Do you work best in small bits of time?

We are all different in our patterns. It will serve you well to know your own.

Suppose you like the idea of long chunks of time, but when you block that large amount of time in your schedule, you don't use it as efficiently as you could. Instead you **fritter** some of that available time.

I like the word "fritter", because it aptly describes how we often use our time ineffectively. Very few of us are diligently focused every minute of every hour.

For example, imagine you have a project that will take three hours to complete.

Do you just begin at the beginning or do you take time to plan out how best to use those three hours?

What would happen if you took the first fifteen minutes for planning time? Would the balance of two hours and forty-five minutes be more productive?

A more detailed intention might look like this if you were working on a book:

◆ Hour 1—Write the introduction.

◆ Hour 2—Create the table of contents with working titles for each chapter and with some subtopic points.

◆ Hour 3—Begin writing the first draft of chapter one.

The strategy is to mentally, in advance, determine your intended accomplishment so that you work at the desired pace and achieve results.

*It is all about your productive mind-set; it is **not** about the clock.*

Example

Ben struggled with not having long uninterrupted stretches of time for his work in the office. He traveled to client offices three out of the five workdays a week. The other two days in the office were for the purposes of preparation for the upcoming client visits and follow-up on the previous client visits.

Every week, Ben would need to create a report for his boss, capturing the key statistics of his activities and results. When Ben tried to create this report during the time he was in the office, he would become very frustrated. He found it challenging to get the report done accurately and completely because of distractions and interruptions.

One day he realized it was taking at least four hours to complete a relatively basic report when done during the middle of the day. Ben decided to come into the office earlier one morning before the rest of the employees arrived, specifically, to work on that report.

In the quiet of the morning with intentional focus on just that task and no interruptions, Ben was able to complete the report in forty-five minutes.

Shifting the time of day he worked on that task made him much more efficient. It minimized the frustration he felt, and eliminated the stress. Now, he had more available time to work on other tasks due to the difference in time between forty-five minutes vs. four hours.

Ben found that it was not a task that could be done in small bursts. He needed the block of time to focus his mind and effort to get it done right.

Learning How Long It Takes to Complete a Task

"The only reason for time is so that everything
doesn't happen at once."

—*Albert Einstein, German physicist*

In general, we do not know how long it takes us to complete a task. We commonly either overestimate or underestimate it. I call this the Time Warp in our Productive Mind™.

This is a key reason our To Do lists do not work very well for us, or that we do not feel caught up.

The normal process in creating a To Do list is to randomly write down tasks we know we need to do. The list might be in an organized notebook, an electronic version or on random scraps of paper. It is a good idea to keep your list in a consistent format and place.

When we captured this information in whatever format, rarely do we assign times to each of those tasks of how long we estimate it will take to complete the task. Even rarer would be for us to actually time the task as we do it. Unless of course you are in a profession where you track tasks and billable hours, then it may be a habit you have already developed.

We might have an inkling of how long it might take if we have done that task repeatedly in the past.

Two examples come to mind:

- ◆ Completing an expense report. A salesperson does this every week or every month. They may have an idea that it takes a specific amount of time to do all the steps and will allocate time accordingly.

- ◆ Getting ready for work in the morning. You know how long it takes from the time you wake up until you are walking out the door to your car. The reason you know how long it takes is that you have been doing it every day. In your mind, there is a time element associated with this.

  You have to be at work at 8 a.m. Your commute takes thirty minutes. This means you have to leave the house at 7:30 a.m. It takes you thirty minutes to get ready, so you have to wake up by 7:00 a.m. Due to the repetition, you know precisely the numbers.

Consider the alternative situation, where you have never done a task before. You have no idea how long it will take or how much time to block out in your calendar. You are truly guessing at this point. If this is a task that will be repeated in the future, then it would be a good idea to time yourself on how long it will take. When you approach the task in the future, you can correctly forecast the time required to complete the task and put into your schedule accurately.

The strategy is to be more intentional in knowing how long it takes to accomplish a task. By so doing, you can more effectively plan your day. The way to do this is to guesstimate the time you think it will take, time yourself as you do the task, and then update the time on paper or in your head for future reference.

Shifting your mind to how long it takes will help you to reduce anxiety or overwhelm. More importantly, once you are aware of how long a task will take consistently, you can then evaluate if the time spent is worthwhile. It may be that you are spending too much time on a task that provides minimal value. Or the reverse situation could occur where you are not spending adequate time to do an excellent job.

Until you are fully aware of the relationship of the task and the actual amount of time, you might be out of balance. It is the Productive Mind™ that recognizes when and where the tweaks will need to occur.

*It is all about your productive mind-set; it is **not** about the clock.*

Example

Kim, a small business owner, provided a service for her clients. I asked her how long it took her to create a proposal for a serious prospect. Her response was that it was four hours to create the proposal to present to the client.

Knowing her business and her hourly rate, I was aghast and wondering how could she be profitable. I asked if she could reduce that unbillable time of preparing a proposal to a smaller number by working more efficiently.

When I asked that question, she realized that I was challenging her to reduce the time. She began using a different estimating method, which she initially balked at because she wasn't used to it. It was out of her comfort zone. She was afraid she would underestimate her time and lose money.

The reality set in when she asked herself, "How much time was I "losing" on the four hour method **now**?"

For the first two projects using a shorter method of creating a proposal, she did underestimate her time. But on the third one and those that followed, she spent much less time and was more accurate in her proposals. Her proposal creation time went from four hours to about a half hour, saving her a significant amount of time.

If we had not had the discussion, she would be doing the same process that she had always done. Instead, she was willing to adopt a productive mindset to reduce the time by 75%.

Another client, Diane kept putting off writing the marketing content for her web pages, claiming that she simply did not have time.

Me: "Well, how long do you think it will take?"

Diane: "At least six hours"

Me: "How do you know that?"

Diane: "I am not sure. It is just an estimate."

She was guessing. She had not written content for a website before, so she did not have actual experience to draw upon. She was fearful about getting started as she simply did not know how long it would take to complete.

There are a couple of challenges in this scenario. If she was going to approach the project wanting a full six hours to work on it before starting, then that may be a challenge. A full six hour block of time is not always available. Being able to focus and concentrate for the full six hours can also be a challenge.

How was she going to plan out the six hours? Suppose she mapped out two hours at a time in her calendar for three different days.

We need to capture in our heads why we think a task will take a certain amount of time, then capture how long it takes us to get that task completed. By doing so, we can better forecast in the future when we are faced doing that same task again. Then our mind-set can be based on data, rather than a guesstimate.

Why Time Boxing Works and How To Master It

"Nothing in business is so valuable as time."
—*John H. Patterson, American industrialist*

According to Wikipedia, the definition of time boxing is that it allocates a fixed time period to each planned activity. The technique is used to break tasks in a smaller time frame, with specific deliverables and deadlines.

If you are not incorporating the technique of time boxing into your daily routine, you should be.

Learning the technique and shifting your mind on how to use it best as you approach the plan for your tasks. The calendar will fill up with specific tasks you need to achieve.

The main idea behind this technique is that you determine ***in advance*** how long you want spend doing a task and block that amount of

53

time on the calendar. If done effectively, it boosts your productivity as you work at a pace that is consistent with the allocated time.

*It is all about your productive mind-set; it is **not** about the clock.*

 **Example**

Nicole writes a weekly blog. She allows herself exactly one hour to accomplish this task:

1. Decide on title
2. Check out her "Idea File" for information she has previously gathered
3. Do some research online for content and pictures
4. Begin writing the first draft
5. Proofread
6. Edit
7. Proofread again
8. Post to her WordPress site

Her blogs are approximately 500 words long, using Microsoft Word.

As she begins, she sets the timer for one hour and begins. By doing so, she stays focused on the eight steps to complete her blog. Using an old-fashioned timer, she hears the ticking of the timer and incorporating another sense in addition to sight and touch, reminding her to stay focused to get the job done in one hour.

When Nicole did not do time boxing, she would be distract herself doing other activities such as Internet surfing, answering the phone, working on e-mails, or other tasks except for the one she really wanted to accomplish. To finish her blog, it used to take her three to four hours. Now, it is only one hour. Now, she has two or three hours of available time to catch up with other tasks.

The other benefit is that by time boxing, she knows that her blog will, in fact, get done every week because she has blocked that time on her calendar. She honors the appointment with herself to get this task done. As a result, she consistently blogs. The mind shift to using this time management technique has impacted her success rate.

THE CLOCK
KEEPS
TICKING

"Learn to build solid processes that
run without your attention."

—*Ben Franklin, author, printer, politician*

We know that we cannot stop time. How we use every waking hour in each day to accomplish what is important to us does matter. Our mind shift is the intentional choice of our options.

Two scenarios come to mind.

First, we know what we have to accomplish. We have the time available to work on a task, but we choose not to. We know we need to do it. Our mind and our actions are allowing us to do other tasks instead.

It is our choice as to how we allocate our time. The mind shift begins with using the available time for what matters most right now.

Second, there is simply TOO much to accomplish in the available time and now we need to be diligent in saying NO to something, so that we can say YES to what is most important.

In either of these situations, it is imperative to have clarity of what needs to be done, what is the priority, and in what sequence the parts of the task need to be done.

We have no influence on time. The clock will keep ticking no matter what. We decide what we want to be caught up on and the amount of time to do so.

It is up to us to choose:

- ◆ A clear picture of WHAT needs to be done
- ◆ HOW important is it
- ◆ In WHAT sequence does it need to be done

Let me introduce you to Nancy, a client of mine who wants to write two books. The content of these books has been in her head for years. She believes these books would enhance her reputation and credibility in her industry: real estate.

Nancy has been in her industry for over twenty years, and she knows these books will enhance her visibility and marketing efforts. She views the book as a fancy business card filled with valuable information to help her clients.

The crazy season to sell houses is from March to October, thus allowing for some downtime during the four-month period of November through February.

To realize her dream, Nancy was determined to write one of the books during the down season. She hoped that she could accomplish her goal during those four months. Otherwise, she knew that another season would go by and her dream of being an author would not have been realized.

The clock keeps on ticking.

So in 2015, Nancy made the choice on how best to use her time during the down season. She became more intentional about her available time. She promised herself that she was not going to let another year go by without accomplishing this goal. She said NO to extra activities that she would have normally done: networking groups, serving on clubs' committees, or working on new marketing campaigns for her business.

Instead, she blocked out time each day to begin writing the book. She broke the task down into increments she could manage of writing at least 500 words per day; at least four days a week.

At the end of the four months' time, she had completed her first manuscript, approximately 25,000 words. Her strong desire to complete the larger task broken into manageable chunks outweighed the smaller, less significant tasks she could have completed.

The time-management techniques were important to getting the task done. But, the mind shift of choice, the belief in herself that she could take on and finish this task built up her confidence. She sustained her efforts, day after day. Her book was published. **Bottom of Form**

Awareness of the Various Clocks in Your Head

"I know the price of success: dedication, hard work, and an unremitting devotion to the things you want to see happen."

—*Frank Lloyd Wright, architect, writer, educator*

When I give presentations on productivity, I show a series of fun slides purposely designed to elicit a laugh from the audience. I could not describe these slides as well as I could show you. Each of us has our individual thoughts about time.

- ◆ Internal Clock
- ◆ Fuzzy Time Clock where time gets away from us
- ◆ The Now Clock where everything must be done NOW
- ◆ The Deadline Clock never stops; time doesn't stop.
- ◆ The Juggling-Time Clock with too much to do and feeling like you are always juggling time

◆ The Procrastination clock — more time in the beginning; squeezes at the end.

Managing all those clocks in our head is what exhausts us, along with the incredible amount of information we must absorb every day. Being aware of the clocks in our head and how they got there will assist you in managing and staying on top of them. All of these clocks in our head contribute to the concept of being behind or being caught up.

Our Internal clock: Our view of time starts when we are young, beginning with our environment, how our parents viewed time, and our own wiring on how we think about time.

Our Fuzzy clock: This warped send of time happens when we have no idea what time it is. Sometimes we get involved in tasks and simply lose track of time. Time passes by so quickly when we are "in the flow" of the moment(s). Logically, we know that each minute is of equal measurement. Emotionally, we don't care what time it is.

Our Now clock: Urgency becomes a function of our belief system or someone else's. We feel compelled to do this task now. What is driving us is not about the clock, but rather it's about what is in our mind. We may work for someone who believes that everything has to done NOW, with no sense of priority. To them everything is a priority. Logically, we know that cannot be true. Emotionally, we feel pressured to perform.

The Deadline clock: We know we have tasks to get done. We know the clock is ticking. Sometimes that knowledge helps us to pick up the pace and move faster. Sometimes we feel pressured that we do not have enough time to accomplish what we want to get done. Logically, we know we cannot stop time. Emotionally, we become anxious and freeze up.

The Juggling-Time clock: We have a lot to do. We attempt to multitask. We spend a little time on a lot of things. We think we are making progress. Maybe we are; maybe we are not. We bargain with others to "buy more time." Logically, we convince ourselves we are making progress. Emotionally, we feel overwhelmed and feel as though we are behind with too much to do.

The Procrastination clock: This is my favorite clock. We commit to something that is three weeks away. In our minds, we have a lot of time, so there's no need to work on it or worry about it right now. Then all of a sudden, we have one day or one hour before that commitment is due. Yikes, where did the time go? The hours feel compressed. Logically, we know that each minute is sixty seconds, that each hour is sixty minutes, that each day is twenty-four hours. Emotionally, we feel time has compressed as we frantically try to get done what we promised.

What additional clocks do you have in your head?

*It is all about your productive mind-set; it is **not** about the clock.*

 # Example

Donald, a co-worker, had two speeds: slow and slower. He was a methodical worker who took his time to do the job right. If you gave Donald a task and a deadline, you knew he would complete the work with complete accuracy. However, your deadline did not matter.

He would not commit to a deadline. You would receive the work when he felt he was done.

He did not know what the Now clock looked like. His clock was the Fuzzy Clock. He worked on a task and completed it when he believed he was done. Whatever he worked on would be accurate and complete the first time. Donald rarely needed to redo his work.

Schedule Your Thinking Time

"To think is easy. To act is difficult.
To act as one thinks is the most difficult."

—*Johann Wolfgang von Goethe, German writer*

"If everyone is thinking alike,
then no one is thinking."

—*Benjamin Franklin, author, printer, politician*

"Plans are nothing; planning is everything."

—*Dwight D. Eisenhower, 34th U.S. President,
5 star General*

To think deeply and with substance, you have to allocate time to do so. No interruptions. No distractions. This is the time when you listen to the wisdom and self-talk in your head. You pose a question or topic to yourself. Usually it is an important one.

The key is to dedicate a block of time on your calendar when you can think effectively.

How developed are your thinking skills?

What is going on in your life that you need to take time to think about?

Block out that time on your calendar now.

If you are behind in your tasks, then spend thinking time to figure out what is contributing to the overload of the schedule. Visualize a funnel capturing your tasks. Input goes in at the top; output comes out of the bottom.

Faster flow with normal pace

Are there too many incoming tasks with too little time to complete? Think of this as a funnel where the top of the funnel is very wide and the bottom tip is very small. The tasks fill up the body of the funnel but only a few trickle out. The feeling is that there is just too much to do or that you are never caught up.

Is it possible to minimize the number of incoming tasks?

Is it possible to match the time needed for the tasks to equal the available time for an even flow of output?

Normal flow but slower pace

Is there a normal amount of tasks but since they are new to you, it takes a longer amount of time to complete? Given the newness and slower pace, is it possible to delay other routine tasks allowing you time to dedicate to these new tasks? The learning curve takes time. However, with repetition, the time to complete a task will become shorter.

Get clarity on what is happening for you.

*It is all about your productive mind-set; it is **not** about the clock.*

 # Example

In 2015, I downsized my living space from a five-bedroom house to a three-bedroom apartment. As you can imagine, it was not a casual decision. Many factors went into the decision.

I scheduled thinking time with myself to consider all the ramifications: the impact on myself and business, the impact on my kids, the financial costs to move, the process of selling the house, and the process of finding a new place. The To Do List seemed endless.

By taking the time to think through the entire project, I was able to impact the execution time. I did not have to constantly re-think decisions. I knew my plan based on the thinking I had done. The time I spent strategizing and planning paid off in a successful move.

All of us are faced with decisions every day. Some big, some small. Honor your thinking time.

Know Your Daily Capacity

> "Striving for perfection is the greatest stopper there is.
> You'll be afraid you can't achieve it. It is your excuse
> for yourself not doing anything. Instead, strive for
> excellence, doing your best."
>
> —*Sir Laurence Olivier, English actor*

> "We shall never have more time. We have, and have
> always had, all the time there is. No object is served
> in waiting until next week or even until tomorrow.
> Keep going … Concentrate on something useful."
>
> —*Arnold Bennett, English writer*

Have you ever had the feeling of having SO much on your plate that even one minor request turned you into a raving lunatic?

It can feel like this:

My To Do list is overflowing.

I am working as fast as I possibly can. I feel so behind.

I am overwhelmed.

My head is a funnel where the tasks are pouring in at a furious pace on the top.

Some tasks are getting done and coming out of the bottom.

But the inflow of tasks is so great that they just don't get done in a timely fashion.

If one more person asks me to put something on my list, my head will explode.

I will reluctantly say yes … but not really mean it.

I will add the requested task to my list and hope I will find time to honor my commitment.

I know in my heart that it truly is at the bottom of the list and not likely to get done on time.

Simply, there are more important things I must do before I even THINK about starting that project.

The concept of knowing your capacity of time on a daily basis is powerful to your mental well-being.

As you approach each day, determine how much open capacity of time you have to accomplish goals on your To Do list. You might plan the night before or the morning of that day.

The recommended steps are as follows:

1. Look at what are your committed appointments for the day.

2. Consider the open spaces of time available to you.

3. Look at your Master To Do list to determine what is important to accomplish that day. The KEY is to only add in those tasks you know that you can actually accomplish based on the time you realistically have available.

4. When adding those tasks to your calendar, assign the amount of time it will take to complete each one.

The mindset shift is accepting that you cannot do all the tasks that reside on the Master To Do List. That list is merely a collection tool of ALL that needs to be done. Ideally, it is on paper or an electronic version and not in your head. Why set yourself up to fail by adding in too much?

You want to feel caught up with what needs to be accomplished today. Overcommitting for today is what makes us feel behind. Mastering this one strategy can have a huge impact on your Productive Mind™ to minimize the "never caught up" feeling.

Your daily calendar and planning sheet (see the Capacity Sheet in the appendix) are your tools to figure out what to accomplish TODAY.

*It is all about your productive mind-set; it is **not** about the clock.*

Example

Gina consistently felt like she was overwhelmed and behind with all that tasks that she had to do. Each day, she would look at this massive To Do list and think "How am I supposed to accomplish all these things in the time I have available today?"

She felt deflated and demotivated on a daily basis. She had two to do lists, one was her personal tasks and one was for her work.

At work, she had conference calls with other employees and clients. Gina had meetings to attend every day. Some of those were meetings that occurred every week, and some were impromptu.

When she looked closely at her calendar, she realized that she had only five to ten hours per week to do any focused work. Those meetings she attended would generate work that she was responsible to do after the meeting had happened. Her challenge was finding the time on her schedule between meetings to get that work done in a timely fashion.

Gina began using the Capacity Sheet as a planning tool on a daily basis to decide exactly what she intended to accomplish each day. The main purpose was to map out what she thought she could get done and do it well. The goal was to leave the office each day feeling good about her efforts and results, instead of constantly feeling the weight of unfinished work.

She shifted her belief that she HAD to get everything done each day on her entire To Do List. She accepted that it was just not humanly possible to do that. She now believes in her ability to focus on today and what needs to be done today, knowing there is still many tasks that will be done in the future.

The Productive Mind™ accepts that you work diligently today on what you can affect today.

As a result, she began to use the suggested words with her boss and co-workers, "I don't have the capacity today to do X task, but let me look at my schedule to see when I can get that done for you."

Previously, she would say "Yes" to whatever was asked of her, without consulting her calendar and disappoint others in her lack of delivery.

Her mindset shift was to:

1. Understand exactly what was being requested of her
2. Determine if she was the right person to accomplish the task
3. Evaluate how long it would take her to do the complete task
4. Look at her calendar as to **when** she had available time
5. Figure out if the task would be done in one block of time or several blocks
6. Commit to doing the task and communicate to the requester the completion date
7. Add it to the calendar
8. Do it!

What she found was that she was able to feel more in control of what she accomplished each day. There will always be work that needs to be done. By feeling more confident and not having anxiety, she was able to focus on each task to complete it in the committed time slot.

Implement Start, Stop, and Continue Now

"It's all right to be afraid. You just don't let it stop you from doing your job."

—*Jim Butcher, American author*

"The START is what stops most people."

—*Don Shula, American football cornerback and coach*

"Being busy does not always mean real work. The object of all work is production or accomplishment and to either of these ends, there must be forethought, system, planning, intelligence, and honest purpose, as well as perspiration. Seeming to do is not doing."

—*Thomas Edison, American inventor and businessman*

We are creatures of habit. We add tasks to our daily lives without thinking about them. We just add and add and add tasks to our list. Our mind-set is to do tasks. And then, we do even more tasks.

Does this sound like your life?

From time to time, we need to do a "look back" to review what we have committed to in our personal and work life. There may be tasks we are doing that just don't serve us any longer. Those tasks take up time we could spend on something else.

In my book *Successfully Failing at Procrastination* I have a chapter dedicated to this concept.

Here is an excerpt:

> At least once a year when I led the corporate team, we would do the exercise of Stop, Start, or Continue. We spent time writing down on three pieces of paper:
>
> > what we should stop doing
> >
> > what we should start doing
> >
> > what we should continue doing
>
> We did this as individuals and also as a team. We shared the results with each other to better understand each other's point of view.
>
> Why bother doing this?
>
> Two main reasons this is important:
>
> > First, since we are all creatures of habit, we add tasks and routines to our daily life, without considering the overall impact on our life.
> >
> > In reality, what happens is we keep adding to our things to the To Do list: new tasks, more reports to read, more key stats to gather,

and more projects. Rarely do we eliminate any ongoing task or project. We just keep doing, doing, doing. The list of what we "feel" needs to be accomplished quickly becomes unmanageable.

If you are overwhelmed with little time to do what you want to do, consider all the tasks and routines you do now. Have you ever thought about them, as a whole?

Second, we rarely stop to think about what is working well and what is not working well. Why do we not take the time to think about these two questions? You already know the answer: We are so caught up in the day-to-day activities of life that we just do not dedicate enough thinking time to assess what works and what doesn't.

So how does this exercise help with procrastination?

I can guarantee you that you are doing things that no longer serve you, take up valuable time, and run in autopilot mode. Of the three categories (Stop, Start, Continue), spend some extra time thinking about what you need to STOP doing. Think about something you need to stop doing or can delegate.

Once you commit to yourself that you will stop doing task X, then your next question is ... what should I start?

You can start doing those needed tasks you've procrastinated. Your mind will keep taking on tasks.

The Productive Mind™ shift you want to achieve is to know that there is a breaking point, and some tasks need to be stopped as they are no longer needed. Precious minutes are being dedicated toward something that doesn't matter any longer.

*It is all about your productive mind-set; it is **not** about the clock.*

Example

Peg took over as a leader in the marketing department at a Fortune 500 company. As she familiarized herself with the department, its people, and its routines, she found five different reports that her staff completed each week that were no longer needed.

She totaled the time spent to accomplish the reports: the data gathering, the inputting, the analysis, and the printing. Producing the five reports took a total of fifty-three hours each month. No one had asked the question "Do we need this report?"

Peg challenged the team by asking "What do we need to start?" They had a list of tasks they thought would help them gain market share, but the team had not done them because they did not have enough time. Now they did.

DAILY NON-NEGOTIABLES

"We work not only to produce,
but to give value to time."

—*Eugene Delacroix, French artist*

If we approach each day in the same way in a routine fashion, then we are more likely to succeed. Why? We have taken the "thinking" out of what we do each day.

Your daily non-negotiable list will be different from mine or the person next to you. The key here is to decide what will consistently work for you.

Create a starting point of what is working now in your daily schedule. Ask yourself what is NOT working and needs attention.

An example for one of my clients, Joan, was that she would schedule meetings for a length of time of one hour. She would run from one meeting to the next one hour meeting, as they were generally scheduled back-to-back. The tweak she built into her schedule was to set the meeting time at 45 minutes, rather than 60 minutes, when she had the control over how long the meeting was to be.

By doing so, she was able to have 15 minutes to take a breath, recap notes from the meeting, check in on email, check voicemail or take a bathroom break.

She realized that she **could** intentionally add in those 15 minutes between meetings. Those days ran smoother and were more productive than when the schedule allowed for no breaks.

Joan felt that she was able to stay caught up with the small details during those small open periods of time.

Look at your daily schedule as to where you need to make adjustments that become non-negotiable in creating your routines. Think about what you can do to feel less stressed each day.

Accomplishing Two or Three IMPORTANT Tasks Each Day

"If it is important, you will find a way.
If not, you'll find an excuse."
—*Unknown*

What would it be like to feel good every night when you went to bed, knowing you had a productive day?

You **can** feel this way. I am incredibly passionate about this strategy when I work with people who are extremely overwhelmed. This feeling is possible to achieve. It does take a mindset shift, but you, too, can do this.

Here's how.

Set the intention that you will decide what the 2-3 most important tasks are that **absolutely must be done** *today*.

This decision can be made the night before or first thing in the morning. Oftentimes, we can easily think about numerous things we need to get done. While that may be helpful, some of those tasks are important; others are not critical; some need to be delegated.

What I am referring to is creating the mind-set and ultimately a habit that you set yourself up to do — every day. Create the routine or habit so you would not live your life any other way.

Your mantra becomes:

"What are the 2-3 things I absolutely need to get done today?" Do not skip a day. Every day counts and builds upon the next one.

Write them down or capture them electronically where the list is visible to you throughout the day. Decide when you are adding these into your open slots of your schedule. The important part of this mind shift is evaluate it on a daily basis, *as each day is happening.*

For example, today is Monday. Be concerned with the 2-3 things for today. Do not focus or worry about what are the 2-3 things for Friday. Deal with that thinking on either Thursday night or Friday morning.

The two or three most important things I need to get done today are:

1. _____
2. _____
3. _____

Find a place to write these two or three things down. It could be in your Day-Timer, in your electronic calendar, on a Post-it note, in a log created to capture this daily list.

Consider this concept. If you do this every day, then on a weekly basis you will have accomplished fourteen to twenty-one tasks that were important to you **at that time.** Or on a monthly basis, sixty to ninety tasks that were important to you **at that time.**

Likely, those accomplished tasks during those thirty days will be more than you have intentionally done in the PAST ninety days.

The goals are simply to:

1. Do this every day.

2. Realize that through the small steps you take each day that are important to you, you will get an incredible amount of tasks done.

3. Learn how to discern what is really important on a day-by-day basis.

4. Go to bed each night saying to yourself "It was a productive day because I got X, Y, and Z done. I feel good about myself." Trust me — you will have a much better night's sleep, as a result.

On the website www.Its6ambook.com, there is a Word template you can download and use to log in those two or three things every day, called Celebrate 30 day Accomplishments.

Print it out. Every day, write down the keywords of the 2-3 things you have done each day.

Use it for thirty days. It is powerful to see your two or three important tasks unfold day-by-day, and that you **accomplished them!**

This strategy is a huge confidence builder. As you use this sheet and look at your daily entries, you realize that you are accomplishing important tasks every day.

*It is all about your productive mind-set; it is **not** about the clock.*

Example

Suzy attended my 90 Day Focus for Results™ course, where we discussed this exercise and mind shift. As she reflected on whether she would do it or not, she commented, "This is my SUCCESS SHEET. If I get this much done, day-by-day that would be awesome!"

The power in this exercise is the building of momentum. It convinces your mind that you CAN be productive just focusing on two items per day. Over time, it all adds up.

I checked back with Suzy after the 30-day challenge to see how it went. She had been diligent in her work in this area. She was amazed at how much she accomplished.

Her testimonial was:

> "*I was struggling to prioritize and get focused as I simply had too much to do. So I did as Lauren suggested and just thought about what were the two or three important things I needed to get done in the next twenty-four hours. I found it to be a relief to just think about one day at a time and what I could do during that one day.*
>
> *It worked for me. I shifted my mind to not be overwhelmed but to just work through my list by taking small steps on what was important **at that time**.*"

Making and Keeping Promises to Yourself

"I feel keeping a promise to yourself is a direct
reflection of the love you have for yourself.
I used to make promises to myself and find them
easy to break. Today, I love myself enough to
not only make a promise to myself, but I love
myself enough to keep that promise."

—*Steve Maraboli, Motivational speaker and author*

Making and keeping promises to ourselves impacts our trust
with ourselves. Consider for a moment how important this
concept is as it relates to our self-esteem and self-worth. When we let
ourselves down by not doing what we said we would do for ourselves,
then we feel deflated.

We start out with good intentions. Really we do. Our self-talk is
filled with promises to ourselves of what we want to do. We think we
can get it done. We are confident it will happen.

But, then it doesn't.

The promises we made to ourselves evaporate.

It is the "I **will do X**" that gets us every time.

We reassure ourselves we will do better next time. "I **will** go the gym, starting on Monday." "Next time, I **will** start that report on time so I don't wait until the last minute."

So how do our broken promises to ourselves affect our productivity?

The acronym is PCT.
    P—Passion
    C—Confidence
    T—Trust

We let ourselves off the hook. Our confidence erodes. Trust our own word… no way.

PCT is a common abbreviation for the word percent. Use this acronym to help you remember honoring your promises.

What percent of the time do you keep your promises to yourself?

As you go through the day, be mindful of the promises you make to yourself. Track your follow through on keeping that promise. Being aware of this will provide you an opportunity to do better. Or consider NOT making a promise to yourself that you know you will **not** keep. Both will build your self-confidence.

*It is all about your productive mind-set; it is **not** about the clock.*

Example

John was a chronic over-promiser. He knew that he was. He had good intentions to help out, but his co-workers and clients knew that he rarely kept the promises he made.

Over time, they did not count on him or his word. Over time, it affected his reputation and ability to be promoted.

Matt, his new boss, pointed this out to John that clients were unhappy with him because he did not meet promises. John was surprised at first, but then thought back to specific situations where he had over-promised and under-delivered.

To remedy this, John decided to shift his thinking and actions. Instead of trying to remember the promises he made, he captured them by writing them down in journal book that he took notes in to every meeting and every phone conversation. By doing so, he was **more intentional about** what he could actually do, make the promise and then make a commitment to get it done in the promised time.

Being intentional about his verbal promises helped him to rebuild his reputation.

His co-workers and clients began to trust his word. When that happened, John felt the shift in their interactions with him. Now, he thinks carefully before he makes a promise. When he says the promise, he will immediately write it down and then add it to his schedule to accomplish it.

Building in Purposeful Blank Times into Your Day

> "Millions long for immortality who do
> not know what to do with themselves
> on a rainy Sunday afternoon."
>
> —*Susan Ertz, British writer*

> "Guard well your spare moments. They are like
> uncut diamonds. Discard them and their value
> will never be known. Improve them and they will
> become the brightest gems in a useful life."
>
> —*Ralph Waldo Emerson, American Essayist, Poet*

Have you ever been too scheduled, where there is simply no space in your day at all?

These are the days where you feel like you can hardly breathe. You feel smothered.

Your meetings and your tasks consume every minute while at work. You feel like you are running from situation to situation with no break in between — with no time for even a much-needed bathroom or lunch break.

I work with many clients on this strategy. It seems like everyone wants a "piece of us".

You **are in control** of your schedule more so than you think you are. You can say, "No" or "I will get back to you." Overcommitting is a common trait of people pleasers.

I, too, am always busy with clients, friends, projects, speaking engagements, kids, hobbies, and just life. One day, my friend Sara asked me, "Do you ever just sit on the couch and just do nothing?"

I laughed when I answered, "No, I do not sit on the couch and do nothing, but I need to!"

I am a classic over-scheduler.

Are you?

The three questions to ask ourselves are:

1. Who is imposing all this busyness on us?" (is it ourselves?)

2. Are we really working the **important** things?

3. Are we filling our time with busyness that is *unfulfilling?*

I find that I enjoy being busy and will find tasks to do that do not truly need to be done or could be delegated.

The scheduled breaks in your day allow your Productive Mind™ the opportunity to catch its breath. You will realize what you have accomplished and what still needs to be done.

If you are not allowing some space to occur, then you will continue to feel overwhelm.

When your Productive Mind™ is able to catch its breath, you will be amazed at how productive you can be afterwards.

*It is all about your productive mind-set; it is **not** about the clock.*

 **Example**

Jan is so busy as a real estate agent during her high season. It is not unusual for her to work from 7 a.m. until 10 p.m. There are some days when she will close her computer at midnight. On those hectic days, she will comment, "Yes, today is Monday but it feels like Wednesday because I have already put in sixteen hours of work today."

How many of us are truly burning that proverbial candle at both ends?

When Jan has open time on her calendar, she has no clue what to do with that free time. She is now focused on how to relax during those open times.

Another example is Sue, a busy business owner, who will easily fill her calendar with client or staff meetings. She was working sixty-five to eighty hours a week with no open spaces, either.

The suggested solutions for each of them:

- ◆ Jan — Create a list of fun things to do for when there is free time. Don't feel guilty when you do the fun things.

- ◆ Sue — Block time on her calendar to limit the amount of time worked, from the eighty-hour weeks to a smaller number. Likely there are tasks she is spending time on now that should be eliminated or delegated.

Recently, I saw a sign that said, "I keep hitting the Escape key, but I am still here!" I bought it for a friend of mine. We do not escape from our busyness enough. We need to.

What busyness do you need to escape from?

Another example of my calendar when the days were filled with back to back meetings that seemed to be scheduled on the hour, every hour. In between, I had no down time. I felt like I was on a non-stop tiring treadmill, running so fast that I did not have time to breathe or think.

A shift in my mindset. Some of these meetings I had control over when they were scheduled and for how long.

Two significant changes to my schedule: 1) Block out time on the calendar where I knew I would need to recharge my batteries and 2) Where possible, change my hour long meetings to forty five minutes.

Two things happened. First, I felt less stressed when I knew I had clear time in the calendar. Second, it forced me to be focused during the meeting to not waste time, keep it on track. Now I had fifteen minutes between meetings to spend alone time to recap the meeting, organize my thoughts of what were the to-do's from the meeting, and to clear my mind.

Managing Distractions

"I have trained all my life to not be
distracted by distractions."

—*Nik Wallenda, American high wire artist*

O f all the areas that impede us from accomplishing our tasks, distraction is the mother of all evils.

How watchful are we to protect ourselves from distractions?

Our Productive Mind™ wants to accomplish the tasks but we allow the distractions to derail us.

How can we train our mind to recognize when distractions impact our productivity?

Distractions come in a variety of forms, such as phone calls, someone stopping by your office, the ding of an incoming e-mail, the unplanned tasks that need attention right now, doing Facebook when work should be done, personal calls, last-minute requests, the emergency sick-child call from school and the list goes on and on.

The four types of distractions are: (1) urgent, (2) important, (3) one-time event, and (4) welcome interruption to avoid what we should be doing. If the boss or client needs your attention immediately, then you have to deal with it in an urgent fashion. At the other extreme, you know when you are exhibiting self-distraction behavior when overwhelmed by too much to do and little motivation to get it done.

Three techniques to consider:

1. If you need focused time without interruptions, then plan for it. Close your door, put a sign on the outside saying "1–2 p.m. — Focused Work Underway"; those who need you can wait an hour.

2. Quickly assess the distraction when it occurs to plan your reaction. The options can be: Deal with it, ask the person how long will it take, or ask if you can schedule time to do it in the near future.

3. Turn off your devices' pinging noises for incoming communication (e-mail, messages, calls). Set an alarm to check your device every hour instead of every ten minutes.

After the distraction occurs, it can take us at least fifteen minutes to get back on track mentally. Just ten distractions a day will add up to two to three hours of lost time.

Your Productive Mind™ wants to manage distractions. It needs your conscious help to make it happen.

*It is all about your productive mind-set; it is **not** about the clock.*

 # Example

Diane intended to work on three important projects between 1:00 and 4:00 p.m. one day.

She had the right mind-set and intent to get her work done but did not manage her distractions.

Here's what happened:

- ◆ Two co-workers stopped by to talk to her about their projects during that block of time.

- ◆ E-mail dings caught her attention. She responded to the four e-mails that came in.

- ◆ Then she saw that five other e-mails had come in she hadn't noticed.

- ◆ A phone call came in from someone she needed to talk to.

By the time she was able to bring herself back to attention on her three important projects, it was 3:45 p.m. With fifteen minutes left, she knew she would not be able to make any headway on any of the three projects she wanted to work on.

She felt that yukky feeling of overwhelm and being behind.
Did she **want** to take her work home that night to work on those three projects? No.
Was she extremely frustrated? Yes.
Was she mad at herself? Yes.

The reality was that she was aware that it was external distractions that prevented her from completing her work that day.

So what were the good things that happened?
And what could she have done differently?

The good thing was that she blocked out time to work on the projects. She had the materials she needed at hand. She was ready.

She could have done a few things differently:

1. Assess her time more realistically and ask herself "In three hours, what can I realistically get done?"

   Three big projects may have been too many projects to tackle at one time.

   Instead, she could have taken on one project and created a list of needed steps, taking the first five minutes (1:00–1:05) to plan the time usage for rest of the three hours:

   - "Of the ten steps I have listed here, I can get steps 1–3 done by 2 p.m.

   - Steps 4–7 done by 3 p.m.

   - Steps 8–10 done by 4 p.m."

   By doing that, she would be able to pace herself, matching the tasks to the available time.

2. Set up her environment: Close the door. Post a sign letting her co-workers know that she was doing "Focused Time" from 1:00 to 4:00. Turn off all devices such as e-mail dings, phone dings. Close all apps on the computer.

3. At the end of the three hours, assess how much she accomplished. Determine any next steps and block out on her calendar in similar fashion for the other two projects.

The Daily Connection of Your Calendar with Your Bank Account

> "Your net worth in life is usually determined
> by what remains after your bad habits are
> subtracted from the good ones."
>
> —*Ben Franklin, author, printer, politician*

How you use your time is reflected by what is on your calendar. How you acquire and spend your money is reflected in your bank account.

If you are a business owner, what are the revenue producing activities you doing every day? How can you maximize these on a daily basis and intentionally tie it to the time slots in your calendar. The time spent on those do, in fact, impact your revenue and profits.

If you are an employee, what are the tasks you are doing that have a significant impact on improving your skill level or professional development? Intentionally build time into your calendar to enhance your skill and expertise. The purpose for doing so is to enhance your value to your organization.

Connect time with money in your Productive Mind™.

*It is all about your productive mind-set; it is **not** about the clock.*

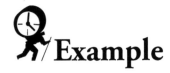 **Example**

A nationally known motivational speaker uses a technique to improve her daily business development habits.

She explained that one of the hardest tasks she has is making outbound prospecting phone calls each day on a consistent basis.

So she creates a game of it by putting thirty coffee beans on one side of the desk. As she makes her calls throughout the day, she moves a bean for each call to the other side of the desk.

A brilliant way to keep herself on track throughout the day to accomplish the dreaded task of prospecting.

YOU CANNOT "MAKE" OR "MANAGE" OR "RUN OUT OF" TIME

"Lost time is never found again."

—*Ben Franklin, author, printer, politician*

We fool ourselves if we think we can control time. Time will pass on its own. The only thing we can control is how we apply ourselves as the minutes tick by.

I know of several individuals who are very careful with their time, what tasks they work on and who they spend time with. I admire their intense focus on how they use their time.

I asked Mary one day as to why she was so good at managing her time. Her response caught me by surprise, but made a lot of sense.

"Lauren, if I stay focused on what I ___have___ to get done, when I ___need___ to get it done, then I will have the available time to do what I want." Having freedom of time to do what she wanted was a huge motivator. It kept her on task with the mundane things she did not want to do. It was her reward!

She explained that there was a time in her life that she had no time for herself as she was working and raising three kids. Mary realized that she had no "me" time in her day. As she looked closer as to why, she realized that she spent more time on some tasks than was necessary to get the job done.

So for the next three weeks, she made a deal with herself to "pick up the pace" on tasks she had planned to get done. She knew she could not "make" time, but she could allot a specific time to concentrate and focus to get the task done.

Soon, she had available "me" time that made her less stressed and happier.

For fun, take a look at Appendix section to see the sheer number of phrases we have in our English language that relate to time and controlling it.

Ask yourself if you use some of these phrases as crutches to support a nonsensical belief system. When you see these words on the pages in their totality, you realize how prevalent "time phrases" are in our everyday language.

Catch yourself when you about to say a "time phrase" that may not make sense!

Identify a Person You Know Who Uses Time Well

"Find someone who has a life that you want and figure out how they got it. Read books, pick your role models wisely. Find out what they did and do it."

—*Lana Del Rey, American singer*

Is there a person in your life who just seems to always have it all together? As you look at their life, you are in awe of all they do. They are productive, successful, always motivated — and they never seem to break a sweat. They are not procrastinators. They are never behind. They are perfect.

What are their secrets?

Have they figured out a recipe that works for them?

It is likely they are hardwired toward activity, as might be demonstrated in their Gallup StrengthsFinder character traits.

If you are not wired that way with traits such as Activator or Focused, then you will need to focus your **conscious** efforts on being productive. Find out their secrets. Experiment to find out which ones will work for you. Adopt their top three into your life. It will make a difference.

My guess is that you will find out from them that it is NOT about time management techniques. Instead, you will discover they have a mindset and discipline about getting tasks done.

Do they have the Productive Mind™?

*It is all about your productive mind-set; it is **not** about the clock.*

 **Example**

I asked my friend Julie on how she seemed to always get everything done, effortlessly. She laughed at my word "effortlessly". She explained her techniques to me. I realized that her magic word was consistency.

Here is what she did on a consistent basis:

1. She took 5-10 minutes each night to look at her calendar for the next day to understand what kind of day it was: crazy busy, normal, or had lots of open spaces, types of appointments, tasks she needed to get done.

2. Based on what kind of day it was going to be, she set her expectation of what she to adjust: adding a few more tasks from the Master List that needed to get done, or subtracting tasks that she did not have the capacity of time to accomplish.

3. She looked hard at how long it was going to take each task and compared it to the time allotted. If that length of time seemed to fit, then all was good. If not, she made the necessary adjustments.

What stood out for me was her key to success which was the consistency of looking at her schedule each evening and being willing to make adjustments.

STRATEGY 17

One Virtue, One Week, Every Quarter

"You may delay, but time will not."

—*Ben Franklin, author, printer, politician*

Ben Franklin, at the age of twenty, created a list of thirteen virtues to live his life by for as long as possible. He focused on one virtue each week and kept a journal on his progress. This was his "Plan" to regulate his conduct.

I like the concept of creating a theme or word to live by each week. You may want to substitute some of the words, but utilize the process. After the thirteen weeks, Franklin began again. He focused on that word for the week. From *The Autobiography of Benjamin Franklin:*

1. Temperance. Eat not to dullness; drink not to elevation.

2. Silence. Speak not but what may benefit others or yourself; avoid trifling conversation.

3. Order. Let all your things have their places; let each part of your business have its time.

4. Resolution. Resolve to perform what you ought; perform without fail what you resolve.

5. Frugality. Make no expense but to do good to others or yourself; i.e., waste nothing.

6. Industry. Lose no time; be always employed in something useful; cut off all unnecessary actions.

7. Sincerity. Use no hurtful deceit; think innocently and justly, and, if you speak, speak accordingly.

8. Justice. Wrong none by doing injuries or omitting the benefits that are your duty.

9. Moderation. Avoid extremes; forbear resenting injuries so much as you think they deserve.

10. Cleanliness. Tolerate no uncleanliness in body, clothes, or habitation.

11. Tranquility. Be not disturbed at trifles, or at accidents common or unavoidable.

12. Chastity. Rarely use venery but for health or offspring, never to dullness, weakness, or the injury of your own or another's peace or reputation.

13. Humility. Imitate Jesus and Socrates.

So how do these thirteen items impact your productivity mind-set? You will find that each of them have a flavor of productivity inherent in the word.

For example, silence. By implementing silence into your day, you will refresh yourself during the time of silence. When you are ready to work, you will be relaxed and ready to be productive.

Incorporate this strategy into your weeks. Impact your feeling of being behind using these words.

*It is all about your productive mind-set; it is **not** about the clock.*

Example

Pat utilized these thirteen words and found they helped with his overall self-discipline. He would write the word for the week in his Day-Timer so he could see it every day as a reminder. Throughout the day, he found that his productivity increased by focusing on that word.

Try it for thirteen weeks to see the impact on your productive mind-set.

Balancing the Proactive and Reactive Day

"Watch your thoughts; they become
words. Watch your words; they become
actions. Watch actions, they become habits.
Watch your habits, they become character.
Watch your character; it becomes your destiny."

—Frank Outlaw, 19th century cowboy and outlaw

Think about what control you have and don't have over your day. As an employee, you have times where you do not have control in order to do your job responsibilities. As a business owner, you react to what needs to be done to keep the business profitable and progressing.

However, there are times in your day where you have complete control of what you work on, who you talk to, what tasks get done. When we know those times with certainty, we can plan accordingly.

Determine when those times occur to maximize what you accomplish.

*It is all about your productive mind-set; it is **not** about the clock.*

Example

During one of my presentations, I brought up this topic and asked the audience to think about what percentage of their day is reactive. One lady in the front row commented that as a customer service rep, her job was to answer the phone and so her answer was 100%. Another lady, who worked at the same company, made the same comment.

I asked if they had to complete work where a high level of focus and concentration was needed. Both said yes. They explained their frustration of having to complete a report every week for their boss that was somewhat complex. With the phones ringing with active customers, it was difficult for them to complete the report accurately and on time.

One of the ideas during this discussion was if they could cover for each other on the phones to allow for 20-30 minutes to focus and complete this important task.

It went from 100% reactive to thinking of how to add in some proactive time. Both women were ecstatic over finding a technique to minimize frustration and feeling behind.

Jump-Start Your Brain Each Day

"Personal productivity is a key differentiator between those who succeed in their chosen field and those who do not."

—*Brian Tracy, speaker, author*

You can intentionally jump-start your brain each day with some intentional actions.

Think about the state of your mind when you begin your workday. You likely have commuted for fifteen to forty-five minutes, navigating the roadways to get to work safely. On your way, you may have thought about the day and tasks ahead. You may have listened to music or motivational information.

A new industry has cropped up called brain training. There are businesses whose mission is to help kids and adults with brainwork. Online games such as Lumosity help with brain development. Go to www.Lumosity.com to see details of how it works.

One of my business owner clients has his two staff members do fifteen minutes of Lumosity brain training games in the morning at the office at the start of their day. The staff swears by it. They say it helps them get in the right frame of mind for productivity.

Learning how to be proficient allows you to quickly be on top of your game.

Study any of the successful people in your field to learn how they achieved their success.

*It is all about your productive mind-set; it is **not** about the clock.*

# Example

Another example of intentional brain training is meditation. It has been proven that individuals are much more productive when they are relaxed rather than anxious.

I observed Camille, an author friend of mine, put herself into a creative mind-set through meditation as she was writing her book. She would work on certain chapters, then stop and meditate to relax her mind. More creative thoughts and ideas would flow to her from the meditative state as she continued her writing

TAKE TIME TO LEARN WHAT NEEDS TO BE DONE

"Productivity is never an accident. It is always
the result of a commitment to excellence,
intelligent planning, and focused effort."

—*Paul J. Meyer, American businessman*

A client of mine, Tonya, was desperate to get many tasks accomplished in her business. As we worked together, I would ask what was blocking her progress on whatever task she hadn't done.

"I did not do it because I did not know how. I did not take the time to learn what to do ... so it was just easier to make excuses that I missed the deadline. It was hard to be honest to say that I did not know how.

"And maybe I really did not want to learn."

How many of us are in that situation? We know we need to do something, but are so crazy-busy that we do not have time to learn the basics.

When we adopt the mind-set that it is okay to not know, then we are open to finding a solution. Being productive does not mean **we** have to do every task. There may be times that our productivity comes from overseeing tasks that others do for us.

Admit that you don't know.

Figure out if you want to learn it.

If you do want to learn it, then:

- ◆ Determine how long of a timeframe to devote to learning it.
- ◆ Remember that you are slower if you are new to the task.
- ◆ Factor that in the learning curve.
- ◆ Be honest in saying I don't know how.
- ◆ Make a commitment to learn.
- ◆ Make a commitment to the deadline of mastery.

A client of mine, John, was creating a new website. He was learning the website software to accomplish his goal. What he found was that he understood the basic website design process, but that it would require a lot more time to add in the advanced graphics, blog information, back end security plug-ins, etc.

He decided that he would outsource the advanced needs to someone who was skilled with this specific website software. The learning curve was too great for him to dedicate hours to it, when he had other more important tasks in his business.

Discover Why Are You Compelled to Do These Tasks?

"Self-confidence comes naturally when your inner life and your outer life are in harmony."

—*Brian Tracy, speaker, author*

Knowing why you're compelled to do certain tasks will help sustain your efforts to start the task and to complete the task.

If the "why" is not compelling, then it will be much easier to lose your desire. When you lose the desire to get the task done, it is easy to avoid or delay its completion. Avoidance is a huge contributor to getting behind.

If you have not figured out the why, then take time to do so. You will find that communicating it to yourself and others around you will help in getting the task accomplished.

*It is all about your productive mind-set; it is **not** about the clock.*

Example

Following through with clients after they bought Jane's services was not one of her strengths. She did not have the money to bring on an assistant to delegate this task. Her clients loved Jane initially, but became frustrated with her lack of follow through.

Some stayed with her service. Some left.

Jane and I met regarding her business, its revenues, and lack of profits. When I asked about her client retention, I could tell this was a sensitive subject for her. She felt bad when her clients would no longer use her services and suspected that it was due to her disorganization and inattentiveness.

We discussed the "why" it was important to stay in touch with them and how to do so in a simple way. Jane created the three steps (a routine) she knew she could follow. For the initial thirteen weeks, of her new system, I held her accountable for getting the follow up done. She created the habit.

Now, she no longer resists doing the follow up as she has had success in keeping her clients longer. She found the positive mind-set and compelling reason to make sure she had time in her calendar.

Find out the Level of Quality Required

"Vision takes a purpose and starts to turn it into
specifics — what specifically will you do, when will
you do it, and how will you accomplish it?"

—Steven Covey, author

It may be possible that some tasks require very detailed attention and accuracy. Some may not.

When you start a task or project, make a judgement as to what level of quality is required.

Likely it is a sliding scale.

Not all work has to be at the 100% level.

If we hold ourselves to that standard, we will be extremely frustrated and spending more time than is required.

*It is all about your productive mind-set; it is **not** about the clock.*

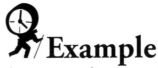 **Example**

Sonia, a business coach, was struggling to get her printed brochure done. She agonized over every word she had written. She was unsure of the graphics she had selected. Sonia wasn't sure if she had the right testimonials.

She felt like she was not progressing in her business networking because the brochure was not done. Every meeting she would go to she would offer apologies to complete strangers she had just met that her brochure outlining her services was not done. She wanted to print 1000 via offset printing to do a mailing.

I asked her the following questions:

1. What is the cost of one brochure? (75 cents to print digitally and 40 cent to print offset)

2. What would happened if she printed up 100 with the information she had, using the digital format — would it create too much anxiety for her? (The cost would be $75 with a brochure that was 80% complete, with a slightly lower standard of quality)

3. Could she use the digital version at networking events and then plan to tweak the information before printing the 1000 for the direct mail project?

She sighed relief, as she had been stuck with her thinking of just one option.

Instead she said, "Yes, I can invest $75, be ok with it, and begin working on the tweaking of the words for the final version."

The point here is that she was holding herself back by wanting it to be 100% perfect.

Sometimes 100% perfect is just not realistic.

STRATEGY 22

When 75% is Good Enough

"Start by doing what's necessary, then what's possible, and suddenly you are doing the impossible."

—*St. Francis of Assisi*

"I think perfectionism is based on the obsessive belief that if you can run carefully enough, hitting each stepping stone just right, you won't have to die. The truth is you will die anyway and that a lot of people who aren't even looking at their feet are going to do a whole lot better than you, and have a lot more fun while they're doing it."

—*Anne Lamott, author*

Have you ever hear that "Perfection is the Enemy"?

Striving for perfection is a fool's game. How will you know when you get there?

Do you have a personality that tends toward keeping you working on a task and then going back to it and working on it again and again and again?

Is there a way you can set a limit of a specific number of times that you work on the same thing?

My limit is three.

When I am preparing a speech or presentation, I will create a rough first draft, usually in handwritten notes.

I then type the chicken scratches I have written into a first draft, do some editing along the way and create a presentation in a Word document. I, then, print out this second draft.

I begin my verbal practice with the printed draft. I will read through it. I will say it out loud.

As I go along, I do make more edits, change words that don't sound right, add new thoughts, and scratch out all the superfluous info.

Then I go back to the computer and type in the edits. (I am calling this version draft 3.)

Then I practice again.

I could be in an endless loop, never satisfied with calling any of it FINAL. But at some point I have to.

Usually I will stop at the third iteration. This version is likely to be 75% good enough. It is my practicing the material that gets it to excellence (above 90% good enough) rather than continuing to wordsmith the drafts to perfection.

What types of projects do you have in your life that you keep going over and over with minimal incremental benefit?

So in the above example, let's say that it takes me a total of three hours to get to the third written draft. Is it worth my time to spend another three hours to get to the sixth draft? Will the work be THAT much better? Likely not.

I need to spend the three additional hours on practicing the already-written words.

You know the significant areas that impact your life and your time.

For some, it might be spending four hours trying to find that missing four cents when reconciling their checkbook.

Is that you?

Would the world come to an end if you made an entry in your checkbook called "X" that adjusted for the four cents, so you don't have to spend that time?

The real question here is "What is the cost of that extra time, in terms of importance or priority?"

In reality, it may be low. If it was $4000 instead of four cents, then obviously that has a much higher importance.

*It is all about your productive mind-set; it is **not** about the clock.*

Example

Mary struggled to finalize the words for her website content. Just getting basic words on paper was hard. I asked her what was holding her back. She was fearful of not getting the right words. She was fearful that others would make fun of what she said on her website. She was fearful that it might not be complete.

I'm her accountability coach. She and I talked about this for at least six weeks. We met weekly for our sessions. Each week, she would promise to get the task done. Each week, she would sheepishly admit she did not quite get it done. She had an outline but not the rest of the words. Also, she had not yet published the website.

Two age-old techniques worked to help her break through.

First, I asked her to answer the question "If no one is coming now to your website, what would be the worst thing that could happen by just publishing what you have done?" (Even though it was not complete.)

Second, I asked her "If you are not able to get all five pages done by next week, could you at least get one done ... to a 75% level?" The technique of breaking the task down into smaller chunks almost always works.

If you are struggling getting something started or finalized, then it is likely the task is "too big" in your head. Thus, the "bigness" stops you from moving forward. Self-awareness of resistance showing up is your clue on the task you are avoiding. The task or project needs to be broken down in your mind or paper into its smaller tasks.

Perfection can be used subconsciously as a way to procrastinate tasks.

We have to find a way to accept that perfection serves us in specific circumstances.

If we look closely enough at our lives, we usually will find that ***The Perfection Mind-Set*** goes back a long way … to our childhood. Generally, we have had this tendency for a long, long time. Most who have this characteristic are very aware of it.

What steps do you need to take to deal with your perfectionistic tendencies?

Using Small Bits of Time Effectively

*"Learn how to use ten minutes intelligently.
It will pay you huge dividends."*

—William A. Irwin, professor

Most of us think that we need huge chunks of time to accomplish tasks.

Sometimes it is hard to find those large chunks of time in our busy schedule.

Instead, we need to consider those ten-minute blocks of time we have, such as waiting between meetings, between phone calls, between picking up children or between tasks.

Some of our tasks take only one or two minutes to complete.

What would happen if you had a ten-minute block and could complete three to five very small tasks?

*It is all about your productive mind-set; it is **not** about the clock.*

Example

Harry is a field sales rep who travels by car to his appointments each day. Many times, he is asked to wait for his client beyond the appointment time. Harry could sit there and play on Facebook or look at a sports update.

Instead, he intentionally puts small tasks he needs to do in his briefcase. By doing so, he is able to spend more time with his family because he does not have to do those small tasks afterhours.

As a result, he feels less stressed and less behind in his tasks.

Impact of Repetitive, Small Steps

"All great masters are chiefly distinguished by the power of adding a second, a third, and perhaps a fourth step in a continuous line. Many a man had taken the first step. With every additional step you enhance immensely the value of your first."

—*Ralph Waldo Emerson, American essayist, poet*

It is in the small steps that we stay focused on the path. Instead of looking for a dramatic breakthrough, we will want to seek the small next steps.

The accomplishments, though small, help us realize we are in fact moving forward, rather than backward.

We need that gentle encouragement, especially on projects that are long in nature or on a task that is complex with many steps.

Instead of viewing the small steps as annoying … we should honor them.

Think of how easy it is to schedule and do a few steps toward a bigger task.

The challenge is the self-discipline required to commit to those small steps.

*It is all about your productive mind-set; it is **not** about the clock.*

Example

I work with individuals who want to be high achievers. As part of the process, I ask them to complete a progress page at the end of every week to capture their accomplishments.

In the beginning, many resist doing it. I insist it be done anyway.

About the third or fourth week, they begin to get in the habit of blocking time on Friday afternoon or Sunday night to do it.

They look back on the week that just happened: What went well, what needed improvement, key accomplishments, key lessons learned.

(Anyone interested in receiving a download of my template for recording your weekly reflections, e-mail me at Lauren@LaurenMidgley.com)

They make a quick plan for the upcoming week. What are the major events, appointments, tasks for the week?

Both tasks should take no more than ten minutes to accomplish. Just list the highlights.

It is a small task to do every week.

But the powerful learning that happens when one takes this small step, repeatedly, every week, dramatically improves overall performance.

Why does that happen?

The continual focus.

Let's imagine that this task took two hours instead of ten minutes. Would most people do it? Likely not. But the small step of ten minutes on a consistent basis is extremely powerful in the following ways:

1. Clarity of accomplishments — they just happened so are easy to remember

2. Awareness of what did not get done and why

3. Sense of confidence from the accomplishments

4. Desire to see the accomplishment list continue to grow

Consider this: You'll have fifty-two pages of accomplishment highlights when reviewing the year. Quite helpful to have taken those small steps each week when it comes to performance-appraisal time.

MAKING AN IMMEDIATE DIFFERENCE

"List all the tasks you complete in a day, from the 8 a.m. e-mail check through to the 5 p.m. task review (or whatever it is you do). Everything. Then, using either paper or a mind-mapping tool, group all those tasks together in what seems like a logical match to you. There's no right or wrong, obviously, since whatever your brain is telling you is the way that you think about those tasks."

—Joel Falconer, blogger

We all want changes to happen quickly in our lives.
We want those changes to make an immediate difference.
We want those changes to have significance.

To do so, commitment is required.
Having an open mind to change is required.

It is possible.

Managing Your E-mail Time

"A real decision is measured by the fact that you've taken a new action. If there is no action, you haven't truly decided."

—*Tony Robbins, motivational speaker, author*

E-mail is the primary method of written business communication and not likely to go away any time soon. An incredible number of hours are spent on this communication tool.

Intentionally managing your in-box and out-box will make a difference. Letting e-mails pile up is not a good strategy.

Take time to learn the top five productivity techniques of your e-mail software, whether it is Outlook or Gmail. Most of us have never taken a class on this and probably know only 5-10% of what the software has to offer.

Whether you receive 50 e-mails a day or 500, there is one common axiom. The more e-mails you send, the more e-mails you will receive.

Consider doing these five actions:

1. Set your security settings on High to minimize the spam you receive. Scan your junk-mail folder once a day for any e-mail that you want and should not have ended up in there.

2. When you send an e-mail, write your message in three lines total. Practice brevity for yourself and as a role model for others.

3. Learn the keyboard shortcuts for your software, rather than using the mouse. For example, in Outlook, use:

   ◆ Ctrl N to create new e-mail

   ◆ Alt S to send an e-mail

   ◆ Ctrl R to reply

   ◆ Ctrl P to print

   Just knowing those four commands can speed up your e-mail processing time.

   Once you have mastered those four shortcuts through repetitive use, then take on four more techniques.

4. When processing your e-mail, in Outlook, use Insert if you need to take action today. It will add a red flag signaling that it is a priority and put the e-mail on your Outlook To Do list.

5. Respond to every e-mail within twenty-four hours.

*It is all about your productive mind-set; it is **not** about the clock.*

 # Example

Consider how many hours you spend each day on email.

How many do you receive?

What would life be like if you could minimize the amount of time?

Each person's email challenges are a bit different, ranging from:

- ◆ Receiving too many non-essential emails
- ◆ No time during day to respond promptly
- ◆ Receiving complex emails requiring focused thought and length replies
- ◆ In box overflowing
- ◆ Not using templates to handle routine communication

Managing email is a skill that can be enhanced and developed further. Seek out a class on your email software online for tips and techniques. Learn a few, use for a few weeks, then learn some more.

Be the Follow Through King or Queen

"Being able to quit things that don't work is integral to being a winner."

—Tim Ferriss, author

How can you be the King or Queen of Follow through? You can do this by creating a "Waiting to Hear Back from You" list. Add and subtract from it daily.

How many times do we initiate an action with another person and then do not get a response? It is a common occurrence that we cannot move forward until we hear back from someone else.

We reach out via e-mail or voice mail with our request for their action. The "dropped through the crack" situation sets in.

What happens when you don't hear back from them?

Do you have a rock-solid follow-up system that you implement within a specific time period?

Our productivity can be impacted by others' lack of action. It adds to our feeling of being behind.

It is imperative that we keep track of people we need to hear back from with answers or acknowledgement of finished tasks.

Following up with them helps you progress with *your* tasks.

There are several ways to do this; pick the system that works best for you.

1. Plain sheet of paper, entitled Waiting to Hear Back, with three columns.

   Column One — Who Column Two — What Column Three — By When

   You will need easy access to update this information throughout the day. Keep the sheet near your planning documents.

2. Excel spreadsheet with columns as described in 1.

3. Online electronic tickler file using Google Calendar, OneNote, Outlook, or Evernote. Create the note of who, what, and when. Set the reminder notification.

If others are negatively impacting your productivity effectiveness, then it is up to you to stay on top of the situation with them. Friendly reminders signal to them that you highly value their completion of their part. No follow-up communication to them signals you have no expectation.

*It is all about your productive mind-set; it is **not** about the clock.*

Example

Every Monday morning, Sally was responsible for completing a report for the president of her company. She used input from the field salespeople to compile the dashboard report. If one of the salespeople failed to provide information, then Sally was unable to finalize this task.

In this situation, the report was weekly. The salespeople knew their deadline was the Friday, so that Sally could have it done by Monday. Gathering the data became a habit for all of them.

Suppose someone was consistently late with their information. Sally's productivity and ability to complete the report on time would be affected.

Originally, she had set it up to receive the information early on Monday morning to create the report. Over and over again, she was delayed based on someone not being timely with their information. By moving the deadline to the previous Friday, it reduced her stress and improved her ability to create report.

Know When to Say Yes; Know When to Say No

"No is a complete sentence and so often we forget that. When we don't want to do something we can simply smile and say no. We don't have to explain ourselves, we can just say 'No.' Early on in my journey I found developing the ability to say no expanded my ability to say yes and really mean it. My early attempts at saying no were often far from graceful but with practice even my no came from a place of love. Love yourself enough to be able to say yes or no."

—Susan Gregg, teacher, advisor

Mastering this strategy of being able to say Yes or No requires finesse, understanding of the circumstances and the overall balance of what is possible.

We have all had that situation where we said, "Yes", and meant "No". As soon as the words flew out of our mouth, we had that small inside voice saying to us..."why did you just say Yes?". And vice versa.

Saying Yes or No does impact our time. It impacts whether we have our focus on what we have already committed to or on a request someone asks of us.

Self-awareness on this strategy is crucial. Saying one answer and wishing we had replied differently contributes to our being stressed and being behind.

Before answering, take a pause to think and be honest with yourself. Get comfortable with the truth of saying what you really want to say.

*It is all about your productive mind-set; it is **not** about the clock.*

Example

For most of us, our schedules are overcrowded due to over commitment. We are asked to schedule an appointment or complete a task. Looking at our calendar, we see an open slot, which we fill with the meeting that sounds like a good idea at the time. As the date approaches, we ask ourselves, "Why did I commit to that date?"

Joel struggled with getting his own work done. He had volunteered to be on this cross-functional team that was taking more time than he had anticipated. His projects suffered. Luckily, he had a conversation with his boss to explain the situation so that it did not affect his overall performance review.

Mary did not want to close her door at work for fear it would offend another co-worker. She was more concerned about the feelings of others than about her job performance.

When I said those exact words to her, she realized that she could communicate to her co-workers why she needed to concentrate on her project. It was her way of saying "No" to communicate to her co-workers — do not bother me at this time.

We resent ourselves when we say Yes and would rather say No.

Do you have situations where you said "Yes" and should have said "No"? Is there a way to amend the situation to your favor?

Adopt a 5 Minute Nighttime Ritual

"A sense of the value of time … is an essential
preliminary to efficient work; it is the only
method of avoiding hurry."

—*Arnold Bennett*

What you are doing each night before you go to bed *does* make a difference in your productivity levels and in how well you sleep.

The focus in this section is on your mind-set, on developing the Productive Mind™ as you finish out your day.

Spending five minutes to reflect on what is most important to accomplish the next day is time well spent. Oftentimes, we will think about how much we have to do, how overwhelmed we are, how tired we are, how busy we are — but we rarely will think *intentionally* and with purpose.

We all have our bedtime rituals on winding down the day.

My suggestion is to spend no more than five minutes at the beginning of your wind-down time with your planner. Here is what I suggest you do:

1. Look at your calendar for the next day — your appointments, commitments, and deliverables. In this step, simply take in the big picture. Approximate time: one minute

2. Next, download onto paper or your electronic page whatever is in your head that are unfinished or leftover items from **today**. Capturing them at this point in the day will clear them from your mind and your "worry center." You may find it best to write them down on a blank page. Or it may work best to enter them in your master To Do list. Capture the key words. No need for long explanations. This effort is to remind you of the unfinished or leftover task, event, discussion, and so on. Approximate time: two minutes

3. Now, look over the specifics of tomorrow on your today's task list. Ask yourself two key questions:

   a. Given my appointments and commitments, do I **really** have enough time to accomplish all I plan to get done? If not, simply **circle** those you are unsure of. You will deal with it tomorrow. Tonight you are just thinking and planning, not taking any action.

   b. Highlight and commit to the **two or three most important tasks** you want to accomplish tomorrow. Say this out loud to yourself:

      "Tomorrow, I will get #1 and #2 done. I have the time and desire to make them happen. I know I can do this. I will feel good that I have accomplished #1 and #2".

Approximate time: two minutes.

These three steps accomplished in five minutes bring a positive close to your productive day.

The goal is to frame the next day in your mind as **doable**. Yes, you can do this.

You want to have a positive perspective about the next day **before** you go to bed. Going to bed with a positive feeling about the next day will set the stage for you waking up with a positive viewpoint about the new day.

Do a five-day challenge, starting on Sunday night. Try it out to see if you sleep better each night and have more productive days.

It is worth the five minutes. Trust me.

*It is all about your productive mind-set; it is **not** about the clock.*

Example

George consistently followed the steps in closing down his day. He embraced the concept of releasing the day and all that had gone on. He "programmed" his brain to anticipate that tomorrow would be an amazing day.

Usually, when he woke up, he found that he was ready to take on the day.

Using the Light-Switch Concept to Shut Down the Mind

"There will be another chance waiting for you tomorrow — an opportunity to do better, get it right, start again, and/ or make up for lost time. But right now, the very best thing you can do to get ready for the new day is to rest without worry or concern. And simply trust that the 'getting there' is already underway and won't be stopped."

—*Unknown*

Have you ever had difficulty going to sleep at night due to so many tasks running through your head? Your mind just keeps working overtime and you cannot seem to shut it down.

No matter what you do, the ideas just keep coming. You continue to think about all the tasks you need to do tomorrow. The unfinished tasks from today plague you.

You tell yourself that you must remember all these thoughts in the morning. Mentally, you are completely exhausted. Physically, you are worn out. You know that the hours are ticking away.

The next time this happens, try this strategy out. Visualize a huge light switch that measures at least eight feet tall and five feet wide. Picture yourself getting out of bed, calmly walking over to the light switch, and flicking it from the ON position to the OFF position.

As you do so, tell yourself this:

- "It is time for my mind to go to sleep."
- "I have thought about these tasks enough."
- "The switch and energy are now OFF."

Picture turning away from the light switch and heading back into the bed for rest.

Try this visualization exercise over and over again. You are training your mind to shut down and relax, by using the image of a familiar object for turning off energy. By the third or fourth night, your brain will be ready for this ritual.

Sleep and being well rested are crucial factors in your productivity level for the next day.

When I speak to groups about this concept, I see many heads nodding. Many have tried this technique with success.

*It is all about your productive mind-set; it is **not** about the clock.*

Example

My client, Joan, suffered from having a lack of sleep due to an over-active mind that continued to think about the day. Her coping skills were at an all-time low. Her work performance and relationships suffered.

She worked on her nighttime sleep rituals so that she could obtain a better night's sleep. The light switch visualization helped her immensely, as did quiet activities and journaling right before she turned out the light.

What have you tried in the past that worked? Try doing it again. Your rest is so important to your daytime productivity levels.

Using Three Success Templates: Master and Implement

"The organized person ... makes the most of
his time and goes to bed for the night perfectly
relaxed for rest and renewal."

—*George Matthew Adams, American newspaper columnist*

"At least three times per day at scheduled times, he
had to ask himself the following question: Am I being
productive or just active? Charney captured the essence
of this with less-abstract wording: Am I inventing
things to do to avoid the important? He eliminated
all of the activities he used as crutches and began to
focus on demonstrating results instead of showing
dedication. Dedication is often just meaningless work
in disguise. Be ruthless and cut the fat."

—*Tim Ferriss, Author*

The three success templates can be found at: www.Its6ambook.com for you to download and use. A sample of each are shown in the Appendix.

They are:

- ◆ The Master List
- ◆ The Capacity List
- ◆ The Next 90 Days List

Let's talk about the traditional To Do task list that is the laundry list of all that needs to be done. I believe it is not useful as it could be.

Here's why. Depending on how the list was created, it may just be a brain dump of all the things that need to be done: in the next hour, today, this week, or next week. Using such a list, it is hard to determine priorities. This type of list usually is overwhelming to the person looking at it every day. Just thinking about or deciding what they want to work on today is daunting.

So instead of referring to it as the To Do list which might be construed as what needs to be done today, re-frame how you think of it. Instead, call it a Master List. This brain dump is important as it captures all that needs to be done in one place, eliminating pieces of paper here and there.

Next is the Capacity List, which is a planning tool for what you think you have the capacity to accomplish for a specific day. The list shows twelve or fewer things to do. You would create this list the night before or on that morning of what needs to be accomplished that day, how long you estimate it will take to accomplish these tasks, and the 2-3 most important tasks to get done.

The main purpose of the Capacity List is to determine and plan for how much time is available to you, given existing commitments, unmovable appointments, etc.

For example: If the day is full of meetings, then the capacity to accomplish your other work will be limited. Adjust your mind-set and plan accordingly.

Also, by determining how much time is allocated to each task, you will do two things: (1) work efficiently to complete the task in that time frame and (2) learn the amount of time it takes to do that task. When that task must be done in the future, you will be better able to adequately plan for it.

The same thinking process occurs for the ninety-day view. Planning for the 2-3 most important projects to accomplish each month in The Next 90 Days List helps you stay focused and avoid working on too many things at once.

The overall idea on the three documents is that they support your calendaring system, which could be in paper or electronic format.

*It is all about your productive mind-set; it is **not** about the clock.*

Conclusion

Yes, it is 6 a.m. and I am refreshed and ready to take on the day, excited for all the things ahead of me.

It is 6 p.m. and I leave the office, knowing that I have accomplished what I needed to do for that day.

It is 11 p.m. and I welcome sleep to close out the day.

It is 3 a.m. and I enjoy my restorative sleep.

It is my hope that you have found value from the ideas in this book to take action, to change your mindset and become caught up. The two aspects to achieve success: 1) understand what is occurring in your world that makes you "feel behind" and 2) take specific actions to reduce the backlog and become caught up.

I want you to feel more relaxed, be focused and in control. The saying of "You cannot outwork your work" is true. How you approach your work and To Do list *is* within your control. Similar to a treadmill, you control the speed and the incline.

Life is short. We all have heard those words. When we lose a friend or a loved one, we are reminded that our in-box is never empty as there are always things to do.

Determine what matters most right now for you. Act on those matters.

The Productive Mind™ is a beneficial outlook on one's daily approach, a deliberate and focused way of thinking about accomplishment and personal satisfaction.

Resources

Time Phrases Used Frequently

The more I studied the concepts of *time*, the more I had an interest in the number of phrases we use on a daily basis about "*time*".

See if you use some of these. Then ask yourself if it makes sense to use these statements in your everyday language. *Time* is *time*. The minutes tick by, no matter what. Can we really manage or control *time*?

Make good *time*	Take up *time*
Make up for lost *time*	Tell *time*
Kill *time*	Live on borrowed *time*
Keep *time*	Lost *time*
Invest *time*	It's high *time*
Time flies	In the nick of *time*
Have *time* on my hands	In my spare *time*
Run out of *time*	In no *time*
Serve *time*	In due *time*
Show a good *time*	No *time* to catch my breath
Stall for *time*	*Time* of day
Take your *time*	*Time* of one's life
Take *time* out to do….	*Time* off

Time heals all wounds

Sands of **time**

Stand the test of **time**

Time after **time**

Time bomb

Time has come

Make it to the big **time**

Time is money

Save **time**

Take the **time**

Manage **time**

Gain **time**

Race against **time**

Ahead of **time**

All the **time** in the world

Before **time**

Behind **time**

Bide your **time**

Pressed for **time**

Point in **time**

Pocket of **time**

A hard **time**

A matter of **time**

Better luck next **time**

Down **time**

Face **time**

For the **time** being

Time immemorial

Game **time**

Time is of the essence

Give it **time**

At the present **time**

Mark **time**

Buy **time**

Catch you at a good (sad, bad) **time**

Do **time**

Have **time**

Waste **time**

Fight against **time**

Find **time**

A stitch in **time** saves nine

Give the **time** of day

Pass the **time**

On **time**

Two **time**r

Down for the third **time**

Have a **time** of it

Time to go

Time warp

Time will tell

Times up

When the **time** is ripe

Behind the **time**

In the nick of **time**

All in good **time**

It's about **time**

At a set **time**

On borrowed **time**

Hang **time**

Whale of a **time**

Make it on **time**

In due **time**

From **time** to **time**

Master List

Date Added	What and Why	How Long It Takes	By When √ on Calenda

Capacity To Do List
(DAILY Planning Sheet That Gets Results)

Description	√ Done	Approx Time to Do It	Actual Time To Do it	*Most important tasks to do today

Goal: End the day and be SATISFIED WITH YOUR RESULTS of what was done!

What I need to say NO to, Promises Made, Distractions That Happened	Appointments/Commitments For the Day:

90 Day Goals and Accomplishments

Month	What, Why, Who	Started	Completed

Month	What, Why, Who	Started	Completed

Month	What, Why, Who	Started	Completed

About Lauren Midgley

Lauren Midgley, a business strategist and motivational keynote speaker, is known for her gift to help others get very focused on desired results leading to profits or promotions. She has delivered hundreds of presentations for corporations, associations, business groups, universities and women's groups, inspiring the audiences to think differently about their productivity. Her message is simple, but impactful — **"Know what matters most right now!"**

As a business consultant, she empowers the professionals to become very clear on what needs to be accomplished and in what sequence. Lauren understands what drives people to achieve more than they thought possible. Those she works with are amazed at the impact of clarity and focus to create incredible results in their everyday efforts.

Lauren Midgley is an escapee from the 25+ year corporate life to become the President of her own company, Courage to Succeed Consulting in 2010. She utilizes the wisdom learned at the two Fortune 500 companies where she worked in the sales, marketing and franchise development.

Any organization that wants to develop their people to become impactful, productive leaders needs to hire Lauren for a keynote presentation and/or workshop training.

Visit her website at
www.LaurenMidgley.com

24491262R00097

Made in the USA
San Bernardino, CA
26 September 2015